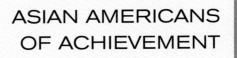

MICHELLE KWAN

ASIAN AMERICANS OF ACHIEVEMENT

Margaret Cho

Daniel Inouye

Michelle Kwan

Bruce Lee

Maya Lin

Yo-Yo Ma

Isamu Noguchi

Amy Tan

Vera Wang

Kristi Yamaguchi

ASIAN AMERICANS
OF ACHIEVEMENT

MICHELLE KWAN

RACHEL A. KOESTLER-GRACK

CHELSEA HOUSE
PUBLISHERS
An imprint of Infobase Publishing

Michelle Kwan

Chelsea House
An imprint of Infobase Publishing
132 West 31st Street
New York, NY 10001

ISBN-13: 978-0-7910-9273-6
ISBN-10: 0-7910-9273-9

Library of Congress Cataloging-in-Publication Data
Koestler-Grack, Rachel A., 1973–
    Michelle Kwan / Rachel A. Koestler-Grack.
        p. cm. — (Asian Americans of achievement)
    Includes bibliographical references and index.
    ISBN 0-7910-9273-9 (hardcover)
1. Kwan, Michelle, 1980–.   2. Figure skaters—United States—Biography.
3. Women figure skaters—United States—Biography.   I. Title.   II. Series.
    GV850.K93K647 2007
    796.91'2092—dc22
    [B]   2006026069

Chelsea House books are available at special discounts when purchased in bulk quantities for businesses, associations, institutions, or sales promotions. Please call our Special Sales Department in New York at (212) 967-8800 or (800) 322-8755.

You can find Chelsea House on the World Wide Web at http://www.chelseahouse.com

Text design by Erika K. Arroyo
Cover design by Ben Peterson

Printed in the United States of America
Bang NMSG 10 9 8 7 6 5 4 3 2

This book is printed on acid-free paper.

All links and Web addresses were checked and verified to be correct at the time of publication. Because of the dynamic nature of the Web, some addresses and links may have changed since publication and may no longer be valid.

CONTENTS

1

Seven Minutes

In January 1998, excitement popped in the crisp, chilly air all over Philadelphia, Pennsylvania. All of the best American skaters had traveled to the City of Brotherly Love to compete in that year's State Farm U.S. Championships. Crowds gathered to watch the skaters practice for their short programs. From time to time, they applauded high-flying jumps and twirling spins. At the end of practice, as the spectators filed out of the Pennsylvania Convention Center, one image stuck out in their minds: champion skater Michelle Kwan crashing to the ice.

After a foot injury late the previous year, Kwan had made some changes to her short program. She replaced her triple toe loop with the more difficult triple flip. The toe loop required her to pick into the ice with her left foot while she leaped into the air. This action put pressure on the stress fracture in her left foot.

On the flip, she picked with her right foot. In order to avoid the stabbing pain to her toe, she and coach Frank Carroll thought the change was best. The only problem was that when she ran through her short program, she often fell on the triple flip. The toe quickly became all the rage in Philadelphia. Every day, Kwan was riddled with questions like, "How's the toe today? Are you thinking of withdrawing?"

Kwan was not planning to withdraw. She simply took ibuprofen for the pain and stuck to just one triple toe loop and one triple salchow in practice each day—doctor's orders. Carroll didn't worry about the falls. "If you're not falling, you're not improving," he said, according to Christine Brennan's book *Edge of Glory.* "When your falling days are over, your skating days are over." He knew Kwan was a feisty competitor and one tough cookie. If anyone could triumph in adversity, it would be her.

Still, many people remembered when Kwan took a devastating tumble during her freeskate in the 1997 Nationals, losing the gold to rival Tara Lipinski. She had fought her way out of the slump, but some remained skeptical. Was Michelle Kwan facing a repeat of last year? Kwan didn't have to compete in the Nationals to have a spot on the 1998 Olympic team. If she wanted one, the U.S. Figure Skating Association would give her a free pass to Nagano, Japan. As the 1996 world champion and the top woman skater in the world in the fall of 1997, she had earned it. But Kwan wouldn't take that road. She wanted to earn a spot on the Olympic team.

On the night of the short program, the air was thick with anticipation. Would Tara Lipinski hold on to her crown as national champion? or would Kwan reclaim her spot as gold medalist? Lipinski skated before Kwan. The famous "jumping bean" took the ice. Lipinski had avoided reporters all week so she could focus on the one thing she was there to do: skate. She was a fierce competitor, there to win. She tore into her program and landed her triple lutz–double loop combination one minute and five seconds into her skate. Next, she prepared for her triple flip. But she rushed the jump and flew into the air off balance. She thudded to the ice and sat there for a second in shock. Lipinski couldn't believe it. For her, jumps were a sure thing, her passion. How could she miss a triple jump? After her program, Lipinski sat slumped on the backstage floor sobbing while her parents and agent tried to comfort her.

Four skaters later, Kwan glided out to the center of the ice. She would have only 2½ minutes to prove she still had the heart of a champion. A couple of nights later, she'd skate another four minutes in the long program. That was it—about seven minutes to show the judges she deserved the gold. Kwan lifted her arms above her head, pretending to hold an imaginary ball.

In previous years, Kwan had performed a spiral at the beginning of the program, then looped around to do the difficult triple lutz. But she wouldn't this time. Carroll and her choreographer Lori Nichol changed this part of her program, too. She'd had trouble landing her triple lutz in the past, and they thought it might be because she had stretched her muscles too long while performing the spiral.

This time, she attacked the triple lutz–double toe combination right at the start. It was a perfect landing. Shortly after, Kwan flew into the air again and beautifully landed the double axel. Less than one minute into her program, she had already performed two delicate landings. "I believe that this short program will be remembered as a signature piece for Kwan," ABC commentator Peggy Fleming said. "It's absolutely extraordinary."

The music grew dramatic, as if it was building up to something. Kwan moved down the ice into her triple flip—the jump Tara Lipinski fell on, and the jump Kwan had been falling on all week in practice. In a split second, she completed it wonderfully. The short program was the technical part of the competition. But when Kwan skated, it was easy for spectators to forget they were watching a short program. All the elements blended together so smoothly and artistically.

Two and a half minutes after her start, Kwan spun to a finish. The crowd jumped to its feet and roared with excitement. Even a few of the judges were moved to tears. "Who said anything about an injury?" commentator Terry Gannon said.

Michelle Kwan performs a jump during the final night of the 1998 U.S. Figure Skating Championships in Philadelphia. Skating to William Alwyn's *Lyra Angelica,* the program was one of her most memorable artistic and technical routines and made her a favorite to win the 1998 Winter Olympics in Nagano, Japan.

Kwan left the ice and sat with Carroll in the "Kiss and Cry" section where skaters and their coaches await the judges' scores and either kiss or cry, sometimes both. Those few minutes seemed like an eternity. Finally, the marks for required elements popped up. They were all 5.9 except for one 5.8. A few seconds later, the presentation scores appeared: 5.9, 6.0, 6.0, 6.0, 6.0, 6.0, 5.9, 6.0, 6.0. Never before in skating history had a woman received even one perfect 6.0 score in the short program at the U.S. National Championships. Kwan had taken seven.

At the end of the night, Tara Lipinski was in fourth place, and Kwan led the pack. Although Lipinski was crushed by her performance, she would still be going to the Olympics. Like Kwan, she was a world champion. There was an unwritten rule in figure skating: World champions go to the Olympics. Besides, Lipinski wasn't out of the running yet; they still had the long program to skate.

CLOUD 9

On Saturday night, January 10, 19,000 people crowded the stands of the CoreStates Center. Six miles away at the Philadelphia Marriott, Michelle Kwan, holding her mother's hand, made her way through the hotel lobby. Her hair was already pinned into a bun, and her makeup was on. Kwan and her parents met Frank Carroll and agent Shep Goldberg, then climbed into a small blue rented Buick sedan. From a distance, the arena was so lit up it glowed. Beams of spotlights disappeared high up in the nighttime sky. Just minutes away, the spotlights waited for her.

There were six skaters in the last group on the final night of the national championships. Skating veteran Nicole Bobek drew the first spot, followed by Tara Lipinski. Kwan would be the second-to-last skater of the night. Technically, Nicole Bobek's program was only mediocre, but she made up for it in artistic presentation. Her scores were enough to win her a spot on the podium and a spot on the Olympic team.

Fifteen-year-old Tara Lipinski was up next. She wasn't thinking about her shaky short program a couple of nights ago. This time, she would be sure to nail every jump. Her first jumps were a bit wobbly, but successful. The larger problem was that she was so concerned with her triple jumps that she ignored her connecting movements. For most of her jumps, she did nothing but prepare for them. The audience was waiting for something more. She managed to pull off her tough triple toe loop–half loop–triple salchow, but she took too much time setting up the elements. When the music stopped, she was still in the middle of a camel spin, a sloppy finish for a skater of her caliber. But she had landed a whopping seven triples and felt elated with her performance. Her scores were strong, better than Nicole Bobek's, and she moved ahead.

Before the spectators in the CoreStates Center and count-less others on television, Kwan stood in her opening stance. She wore a simple ice-blue velvet costume, void of glittering sequins. Nothing would distract from her performance. The only glitter came from the necklace she wore at every competition, a gift from her grandmother. It was a small dragon pendant, a Chi-nese symbol for luck. She soared into the program, landing three flawless triple jumps in a little over a minute. Kwan imagined angels and clouds as she glided through her routine, capturing the heart of the music—*Lyra Angelica*. She continued with the jumps—a triple salchow, a second triple lutz—both magnificent. "She is just breathtaking to watch!" Fleming exclaimed.

With just 15 seconds left, Kwan had one more jump—the triple toe loop. She would have to launch herself off of her bad toe. She had already completed all the required elements, so she didn't need to do it. But Kwan was flying out there on the ice and nothing could stop her from relishing the moment. When she landed the jump, she turned her palms up to the crowd, head held high. It was a spur-of-the-moment move, but it was spectacular. Kwan dropped into a sit spin and twirled up. With only a few notes remaining, she had to choose her finale. A month earlier, according to Brennan's *Edge of Glory*, Nichol had told her "It's your Olympic moment. You do whatever." Kwan simply tipped her head back and threw her arms into the air, making them ripple like streamers above her. Before she was finished, the crowd was already on its feet. The CoreStates Center resounded with deafening cheers.

Moments later, Kwan sat in Kiss and Cry watching the scoreboard. No one thought she could outdo her marks from the short program. When the scores for presentation showed up, they read 6.0, 6.0, 6.0, 6.0, 6.0, 5.9, 6.0, 6.0, 6.0. All but one mark were perfect scores. Since the U.S Figure Skating Championships began in 1914, no long program ever received that many perfect scores. Once again, Kwan had made history. She had also recaptured the gold and her title. Tara Lipinski finished second, and Nicole Bobek took the bronze. At the winners' press conference, a reporter asked Kwan what she was thinking about out on the ice. "I was thinking of angels and clouds and the feeling of flying," she said, according to *Edge of Glory*. "Nothing can stop me. At the end, it's like, 'I'm free. I'm gone. Cloud 9, here I come.' "

After Nationals, Kwan was the favorite to win the gold at the upcoming Olympics in Nagano, Japan. She seemed untouchable. But Kwan's ambitions reached far beyond the Olympics. "I want to be a legend, like Dorothy Hamill and Peggy Fleming," she later told the *New York Times*. "I want to leave a little mark, and have people say 'Michelle Kwan was a great skater, artistically and technically. She had the whole package.' I want people to remember me after 1,000 years when skating is weird and people are doing quintuple jumps." As a nine-time U.S. champion, five-time world champion, and two-time Olympic medalist, she has already made her mark in history. No other figure skater has come close to touching her accomplishments.

Michelle Kwan and her coach, Frank Carroll, react to the announcement of Kwan's perfect 6.0 scores which she earned for her ladies free skate routine at the U.S. Figure Skating Championships on January 10, 1998. During her performance, Kwan flawlessly landed three triple jumps, a triple salchow, two triple lutz, and triple toe loop while suffering from a stress fracture in the second toe of her left foot.

2

"Michelle, Ma Belle"

On July 7, 1980, Estella Kwan gave birth to her third child in Torrance, California. After their first two children, four-year-old Ron and two-year-old Karen, Estella and Danny Kwan decided not to have any more babies. But fate had other ideas for their future. As he gazed down at his new baby girl, Danny was so amazed at how lovely she was that he named his adorable daughter after his favorite song, "Michelle," by the Beatles, about a boy who falls in love with a beautiful girl. The lyrics are "Michelle, ma belle," which is French for "my beautiful Michelle."

Both Danny and Estella Kwan were born in China, but into quite different lives. Estella grew up in Hong Kong, as part of a large family. She excelled in school and loved fine arts such as music and ballet. On the other hand, Danny's early childhood was marred with the struggle to survive in a poor family. He was born in a little village near Canton (today, Guangzhou). His parents were no strangers to the hard life. Danny's father (Michelle's grandfather) was also part of a large family. By the time he was born, there was already not enough food to go around. When he was around five years old, Michelle's grandfather went to work for a wealthy Chinese farmer. For several years, he spent both days and nights watching over a single cow. Eventually, he got married but decided he wanted more for his family than the life of poverty he had known. And so he left the village alone, in search of a better life.

While he was gone, his wife gave birth to Danny. Even as a young child, Danny helped the family as much as he could. Each morning, he rolled out of bed at four o'clock to be first in line to buy a small piece of meat for that day's meal. He was eight years old when he met his father for the first time. Danny's father had moved to Hong Kong and was finally settled enough to bring his family to live there. It was at this time that Danny got a chance to go to school, where he met Estella. Although he later admitted to having a crush on her, they had little in common in those days. Estella was a star student, and Danny, who had a lot of catching up to do, was at the bottom of the class.

At age 13, Danny started working as a messenger and later got a job at the telephone company. The ambitious young man had grand dreams for his future. In 1971, at age 22, he first came to America to attend a family wedding in California. With his own eyes, he saw the country known around the globe as the Land of Opportunity. He decided he could make a good home for his future family in the United States and stayed. At once, he took a job in a restaurant where he learned how to cook. He also worked for a telephone company in Los Angeles. Before long, he and a friend opened their own restaurant—the Golden Pheasant—in Torrance, in Southern California.

Meanwhile, Estella was building a life of her own in Hong Kong. For a time, she worked as a nurse in a hospital. Although she loved taking care of the patients, she couldn't bear to watch them suffer. Before long, she wanted to make a career change; she became a television news anchorwoman. At this point, that

After hearing her scores in the women's short program at the Winter Olympics in Salt Lake City, Michelle enthusiastically celebrates with her father. Danny and Estella Kwan did everything they could to support their daughter's skating career, including working multiple jobs and eventually moving their family closer to better skating facilities.

struggling student she knew in school probably never even crossed her mind—until a class reunion.

Danny came back to Hong Kong for the reunion and found himself captivated by Estella's brains and beauty. They fell in love and got married. In 1975, Danny and his new bride—along with

Danny's mother and father—returned to California, making their home in Rancho Palos Verdes. The whole family pitched in and worked at the Golden Pheasant. The following year, Ron was born, and sister Karen was born two years later. A couple of years later, Michelle Wing became the youngest member of the Kwan family.

Michelle recalls listening to her father tell stories about life in China. At home, the family spoke both Chinese and English. Michelle's parents and grandparents showered her with unconditional love, but she also got doses of old-world discipline. When she was five, Ron introduced Michelle to something that would quickly become her greatest passion: ice skating.

OLYMPIC DREAMS

For Michelle, life really began when she started skating. She doesn't have many memories from before her first trip to Rolling Hills Estates ice skating rink, other than playing with her stuffed animals when Ron and Karen were at school. She and Karen took some gymnastics classes, and Michelle probably would have become a gymnast if Ron hadn't started playing ice hockey.

Soon, Karen followed Ron to the rink, but Michelle had to stay home at first. Her parents thought she was too young to go along with her siblings. Michelle didn't like being left out. She cried and told her parents it wasn't fair that she couldn't go along and have fun, too. Finally, Danny and Estella gave in, and five-year-old Michelle took to the ice. The rink was in a shopping mall in Rolling Hills Estates, near the Kwans' house in Rancho Palos Verdes. At first, they all had wobbly ankles, especially Karen, who Michelle described as having "long flamingo legs" in her autobiography, *Michelle Kwan: Heart of a Champion*. Unable to afford three pairs of skates, the children rented ugly brown ones from the rink that were stiff and hurt their feet. But Michelle didn't care—she was having too much fun skating.

Story of My Family

BIG DREAMS

Like Michelle, Danny and Estella Kwan had big dreams when they were young. In the following excerpt from her autobiography, *Heart of a Champion,* Michelle told the story of her parents' immigration to America.

"My dad started working when he was about thirteen years old. Even then he was ambitious, with big dreams for the future. He was a messenger for a few years, and later got a job working for the telephone company. He first came to America in 1971, when he was twenty-two, to attend a family wedding in California. He saw a chance to make the kind of life he'd always dreamed of, and he decided to stay.

"He started out working in a restaurant, where he learned to cook. . . . Pretty soon, he and a partner opened up their own restaurant, the Golden Pheasant, in Torrance, which is just south of L.A. He worked very hard. He wanted to succeed.

"Meanwhile, my mother was in Hong Kong, working as a nurse in a hospital. She loved taking care of people, but it was hard for her to watch them suffer. She needed a change, and (after thinking it over a lot) she made a big one—she became a television news anchorwoman!

"That's what she was doing the next time she saw my father, when he came home to Hong Kong for their school reunion. And that's when they fell in love.

"Soon they got married and moved back to the United States together. My mother, my father, and both of his parents lived in Torrance, and everybody helped out at the Golden Pheasant. . . .

"We speak a mixture of Chinese and English at home. My father tells lots of stories about the old life in China. I always—even when I skate—wear a necklace that my grandmother gave me. It has a little Chinese dragon on it and a symbol that means good luck. Karen, Ron, and I are very close to our grandparents. Even though they don't speak much English, we understand each other.

(continues)

(continued)

"I've been to China twice—once to skate, not long ago. The first time I was there was when I was very little and my mother took us to Hong Kong to meet her side of the family. I was too young to remember much about that trip now, but Mom always says she's so glad she took us. Just a little while after we were there, her mother—my grandmother—died. It was so nice that she'd seen us and hugged us first.

"But life in China still seems so far away from my life, and so different. Where did my competitive spirit come from? How did my parents end up with a daughter like me, who is so completely into one sport?

"Actually, I can see similarities between what I do and what my parents did in coming to America. They wanted to start a family in a place were they could work hard and keep their kids happy and healthy. America was a faraway dream to them, but they believed in it and made it come true.

"When I was little, my dream of becoming a world-class skater was far away, too. But I learned from my parents that if you work hard enough, your dream just might come true."

Moving to a new country takes courage, emotional strength, and determination. Undoubtedly, Danny and Estella Kwan set a powerful example for their children that anything is possible if they believe dreams can come true. Michelle probably learned to set her goals high at an early age.

The three of them started taking group lessons once a week. "The first thing they taught us was how to fall, which I thought was funny," Michelle later recalled in her autobiography. But the instructors had to teach them how to take a tumble without getting hurt. Then, they taught the kids how to stand, how to hold on to the railing, and finally how to walk on the ice. Little Michelle didn't understand that she needed to learn the basics first and quickly grew impatient. She wanted to be out zipping around on the ice after the first lesson.

Both Karen and Michelle were fast learners. Before long, they were ready for more difficult moves. After just a couple of months, Michelle felt just as comfortable in her skates as she did in her favorite sneakers. There was something about skating that seemed much more exciting to her than padding around on two blade-free feet. "I've always loved the feeling of moving on the ice—the faster the better," Michelle said in her autobiography. "I remember during that first year being the smallest one on the ice and racing around offering Nerds candy to everyone."

Michelle quickly mastered the two maneuvers of basic skating—stroking, or pushing off of one foot, and gliding. Her teachers noticed her natural abilities. After about six months, an instructor pulled Michelle and Karen aside and suggested they take private lessons. By this time, there was little that could keep Michelle away from the ice. She was thrilled at the idea and soon had a regular schedule at the rink. In her private lessons, she learned the basic waltz jump, in which a skater steps forward onto an outside edge and leaps a half turn in the air then lands on the opposite foot on a back outside edge. The waltz jump is the foundation for the axel, which has the same takeoff and landing. Treacherous and risky, the axel—named after its Norwegian creator, Axel Paulson—is the most difficult jump in figure skating. But it would be many more lessons before Michelle would attempt an axel. In these early lessons, she also tried spirals and three-turns. All skaters start with these fundamentals before they can even think about tackling advanced moves such as airplane-looking camel spins, salchows, and what would become Michelle's favorite jump—the lutz. Named after Austrian skater Alois Lutz, this jump starts with one leg skating on an outside edge. Reaching back with the free leg, the skater uses the toe pick to push into the air, does a complete counterclockwise turn, and lands on the opposite foot on a back outside edge. But

this jump, too, had yet to make its debut in young Michelle's career.

In figure skating, being the smallest kid in the bunch had its advantages. Michelle was so light that turning one time in the air took virtually no effort at all. She was so small she didn't need to jump very high to do a full revolution before landing again. As she grew older, she got stronger, which helped her jump higher. Twisting and leaping into the air was an incredible rush for young Michelle. "It was in those days at Rolling Hills Estate that I got my first taste of what it's like to fly," she recalled in her autobiography. But even more than jumping, she loved stroking and gliding around the rink. Sometimes, she would take off across the ice as if it were a runway, the wind blowing back her hair. She felt weightless, like her feet weren't even moving. "Those are the times when I feel most like I'm flying," she said, "when my feet are still on the ground."

From her first lesson, Michelle was always pushing herself to the next level. She couldn't get there fast enough. Skating seemed to be at the front of her mind all of the time. She went to school wearing skating skirts. When she wasn't doing homework, she was daydreaming about her next lesson at the rink.

Then, when she was 7½ years old, something happened that triggered a huge change in Michelle's life. She watched the 1988 Winter Olympics on television. Wide-eyed, she watched the famous "Battle of the Brians," as Brian Boitano of the United States and Brian Orser of Canada fought for the gold. No doubt, she cheered in excitement as Brian Boitano took the men's gold medal. At that point, Michelle decided she wanted to know that feeling for herself. She vowed that one day she too would go to the Olympics.

She began counting the years in her head. At the 1994 Olympics, she would be 13—a teenager. In 1998, she'd be 17; in 2002, she'd be 21. Surely by then, she would have matured into a sophisticated skater. In 2006, she would be 25, older but still young enough to skate. She swore to herself that she would be at all of those Olympics. This promise was not just some childish wish. With her vivid imagination, Michelle could actually see it all happening. As she said in her autobiography, "If I'd ever told myself it was an impossible dream, I never would have gotten this far."

SKATING SISTERS

In those early years, Michelle didn't know what kind of commitment her skating would demand if she was going to make it all the way to the Olympics. At seven years old, she didn't even know a skater had to qualify for the Olympics. She thought she would just have to show up. But she soon learned the cold, hard truth.

When she was about eight, her father hired a new teacher for the girls, Derek James. He taught lessons at a rink in Torrance, just north of Rancho Palos Verdes. In the beginning, Karen and Michelle skated four days a week with James. Before long, it was five days—in the mornings, after school, and on Wednesday nights. The girls rolled out of bed at 4:30 in the morning to be on the ice at 5:30. To catch a few more minutes of sleep, the girls went to bed in their skating clothes so they could just jump out of bed and hop into the car. Some days, Michelle almost complained as she stood shivering on the ice, her muscles aching all over. But then she'd remind herself that she was only there because she wanted to be. Nobody was making her do it. She'd suddenly straighten up, narrow her eyes in determination, and skate with even more energy.

Skating demanded a strong commitment from Danny and Estella as well. When they saw how serious Karen and Michelle actually were about skating, they offered their full support. Over the years, they had to learn just as much about the sport as the girls did. From the beginning, according to Michelle's autobiography, *Heart of a Champion*, they gave their children this advice: "Work hard, be yourself, and have fun." These simple words became Michelle's motto, but she also admitted they were

Michelle Kwan, and her sister, Karen, pose in January 1995 with their coach Frank Carroll in Lake Arrowhead, California. Kwan began working with Frank Carroll in 1992. It was a relationship that would last for the next 10 years.

a lot easier to say than do. The Kwans couldn't always afford to pay for lessons with Derek. At times, the girls had to practice on their own. Both parents had second jobs to help bring in some extra money. Danny still worked at the phone company, and Estella took a job at a factory for a while.

The whole family pulled together and made sacrifices. The girls wore hand-me-down clothes that had already gone through three cousins. They also shared each other's skating tights. One Christmas, Danny told the kids he wouldn't be able to buy a Christmas tree. He reasoned that the tree would only live a couple of weeks anyway, so they could do without it. Michelle just couldn't imagine Christmas without a tree. Perhaps she felt partly responsible for her family's money problems because she decided to take matters into her own hands. She entered a school popcorn-stringing contest. The student who could string the longest rope of popcorn in one minute won a fully decorated miniature tree. Michelle put her heartfelt determination to work and won.

In those early years of skating, Michelle's brother, Ron, probably sacrificed the most. Not only did he have to give up a lot of things that other kids could have, he sacrificed a good deal of his parents' attention. Years later, he would refer to them as "the famous Kwan sisters" and joke that nobody even knew they had a brother, Michelle said in her autobiography. But Michelle and Karen didn't see it that way; they called him Ronald the Great. And after all, if it hadn't been for Ron, they might have never gotten into skating.

After a few months of lessons with Derek James, Michelle and Karen started competing at local rinks and skating clubs. At her first competition, when her name was called, she took swift strides toward the center of the rink and suddenly lost her balance. But she wasn't about to let that embarrassing mishap discourage her. Before long, she was winning her competitions.

The Kwan sisters became quite famous locally. At the rink, skaters called them "Big Kwan" and "Little Kwan." These nicknames were fitting not only because of their ages; Karen was several inches taller than Michelle as well. In any case, both sisters excelled at competitions. Sometimes Karen would win. Other times Michelle would. But usually, one of the Kwan sisters would finish a champion.

At the same time, the girls were taking skating tests to advance to higher levels in the Ice Skating Institute of America (ISIA) and the United States Figure Skating Association (USFSA), the national governing body for figure skating. Sometimes they would compete at different levels, and sometimes at the same level. Being older, Karen would often take a test and move up to a higher level first. But not long after, Michelle would catch up and they'd be even again for a while. Michelle never felt like the two sisters were competitive toward each other. They were more like buddies than rivals. They spent most of their time together, which was on the ice—morning and evening. Their incredible bond, however, stretched beyond their mutual love for skating. In bed, they whispered under the covers. At the rink, they gave each other advice and support.

As much as they had in common, Karen and Michelle were also different in many ways. Karen was elegant and taller. With her slender body and long legs, she looked great in almost everything, from miniskirts to long pencil skirts, and funky, trendy clothes. Being short, Michelle couldn't wear all of the hip fashions and soon gave up trying to dress like her sister. Her style instead was more classic and simple.

It was the same on the ice. When they were young, Michelle watched Karen gracefully dance across the ice like a ballerina. She wished she could put that kind of feeling into her own skating. But Michelle's style was more athletic and aggressive, skating swiftly and confidently, not afraid to lean deeply into her edges, backward or forward. And it was this confidence that would soon catapult her above the rest.

As a young skater, Michelle's greatest thrills came from moving up to a new level in the USFSA. Each level brought her one step closer to becoming a senior lady, the bracket she would need to belong to in order to compete with the best skaters in the world. But there were many levels to complete first: pre-preliminary, preliminary, pre-juvenile, juvenile, intermediate, novice, and junior. In each division, Michelle had to master certain skill requirements before she could move ahead. Every time she advanced, Michelle earned a shiny little pin and faced challenging new competitors.

3

Ice Castle

By 1992, Karen and Michelle had become junior skaters. The excitement Kwan felt at this point was intense. Her dream of becoming a senior skater was within reach. By this time, Michelle had already learned most of the triple jumps, even the tricky lutz and the flip—two of the most difficult moves that women skaters attempt.

After achieving junior level, Michelle needed more than five days on the ice. The Torrance rink had hockey on the weekends, so her parents came up with another idea. The Kwans had some friends who lived in the San Bernadino Mountains at Lake Arrowhead, about 100 miles outside of Los Angeles. The world-famous ice skating facility Ice Castle is located here, and it was open seven days a week. So Michelle's parents started driving the girls there on the weekends. Ice Castle has two rinks—a public rink where anyone can skate and a separate rink for elite skaters. At this point, Michelle could only skate at the public rink. But she didn't seem to mind much. The atmosphere was enchanting at Ice Castle. Towering pines peeked over the walls of the rink as Michelle glided across the ice, practicing her jumps and twists.

Just a short drive down the main street in Lake Arrowhead, a narrow road winds up a hill to a world-class training facility. Only the best skaters from around the world and kids working

ICE CASTLE INTERNATIONAL TRAINING CENTER

The grand Ice Castle rink—in Southern California's San Bernadino Mountains—was founded by Walter Probst and his wife, Carol Caverly Probst. Carol once skated in the ice skating entertainment show called Ice Follies, which ran from 1936 to 1966. For elite skaters only, Ice Castle's enormous 85-foot-by-185-foot rink is encircled by a rubberized floor but has no hockey boards (the waist-high walls that surround most rinks) around it. The rink is open and spacious—a skater can step right off the floor onto the ice. On one wall, a ballet-style mirror stretches from floor to ceiling, allowing skaters to evaluate their techniques and choreography. Parents and visitors may watch from the other end but must stay in their designated area at all times. This way, coaches can work with their students without being interrupted.

Even though it is not a contact sport, figure skating can be dangerous. Fancy jumps and twirls take much practice, and falling on solid ice can leave quite a bruise—if not a gaping cut or broken ankle. Ice Castle has installed a safety harness to protect skaters while they train. The harness hangs down from the ceiling and slides across the entire length of the ice. When learning new and difficult jumps, like the triple axel, skaters strap themselves into the harness so they don't get hurt.

While summer tends to be busier than winter at Ice Castle, at almost any time of the year skaters can be found whirling around the rink throughout the day. Serious skaters have three or more practice sessions each day. They still might spend more time practicing on their own. For Olympic dreamers like Michelle, Ice Castle is a utopia, where a skater's goals can soar to new heights.

with Ice Castle coaches can use it. World champion Lu Chen and European champion Surya Bonaly both trained at Ice Castle International Training Center, as well as many other top-level skaters. Being so close to these great skaters inspired Michelle. Even though she wasn't at their level yet, she was dying to skate with them. "I was so excited every time I arrived in Lake Arrowhead," Michelle remembered in *Heart of a Champion*, "because I felt close to my skating dreams." Then, things suddenly began to fall into place for Michelle, bringing her much closer to her skating heroes.

In 1992, Michelle had an amazing season. She won the gold medal at the Southwest Pacific Regionals, which took her to the Pacific Coast Sectionals where she took the bronze. This medal qualified her for her first national competition—the Junior Nationals. Michelle had already watched Karen compete in a national competition at the novice level. Now, it was her turn. But all the excitement was overshadowed by a big problem—Michelle didn't have a coach. For the past nine months, the Kwans were unable to afford a coach for the girls. Michelle wondered how she could possibly prepare herself for Junior Nationals.

Then, a kind of miracle happened just when Michelle needed one the most. Virginia Fratianne, the mother of world champion and Olympic figure skater Linda Fratianne, had watched Michelle skate at Ice Castle and at some competitions. When she heard about Michelle's spot in the Nationals, she went to Linda's coach. Frank Carroll was considered one of the greatest coaches in the world. One of his specialties was teaching triple jumps. Linda Fratianne was one of the first women to successfully perform triple jumps. But Carroll's skills went beyond teaching girls how to skate. He understood the entire world of figure skating. Once a skater himself, he was a veteran in dealing with choreographers, judges, parents, and the press. Still, Carroll was a picky coach and wouldn't teach just anyone. For instance, Carroll wouldn't bother teaching fancy jumps to an older skater. "To get that body in the air and make three turns, I'm afraid you've got to start them very

Michelle practices with her coach, Frank Carroll, in January 1994. That year, Michelle won the World Junior title and finished second in the U.S. Championships. Kwan also traveled to the Lillehammer, Norway, to serve as an alternate skater at the Winter Olympics. Although she did not get a chance to skate, Michelle started to make a name for herself in the skating world.

young," Carroll remarked, according to Edward Z. Epstein's *Born to Skate: The Michelle Kwan Story*. "If you wait until they're sixteen or seventeen, it's too late." Luckily, one thing Kwan certainly didn't have to worry about was being too old. Virginia Fratianne explained the Kwans' situation to Carroll, and he agreed to give both Karen and Michelle a lesson, as a sort of audition to see if he wanted to work with them.

During her audition, Michelle's heart fluttered nervously. She really wanted to impress Carroll. She knew that he would watch her every move carefully. In the back of her mind, she wondered if she actually belonged with the top skaters. But her doubts didn't shadow her performance. She skated beautifully and was natural and confident. Just by watching her that first time, Carroll knew Michelle had the potential to become a world champion. He agreed to take Michelle and Karen as students. With the Junior Nationals only three weeks away, Michelle knew there would be tough work ahead. But she had no idea what it was like to train as a serious skater. She was about to get her first dose of skating with the top dogs.

A PAINFUL LESSON

A whole new world opened up for the entire Kwan family. Not only were the girls now accepted as students at the private Ice Castle rink, but they also got scholarships to cover much of their expenses. They would live at Ice Castle all year long. They would eat and sleep there and would skate there seven days a week. For Michelle, it was a dream come true.

At first glance, the Ice Castle facility is overwhelming. Having once been a camp, there are 24 cabins. There is a huge dormitory that can sleep more than 70 kids, a 3,000-square-foot dance pavilion, a swimming pool, a Jacuzzi, a gym, and of course the impressive indoor rink. The facility is tucked high in the mountains, 5,400 feet above sea level, surrounded by giant cedars and pines that during the winter months sag under the heavy weight of snow. Peaceful and serene, it is the perfect spot for serious work.

Every day, Michelle attended practice sessions where groups of skaters worked with their coaches or skated alone. Most of the year, the ice was pretty open. But during summer, there were a lot more skaters, and Michelle had to watch where she was going so she wouldn't crash into anyone. Three times a day, the elite skaters held 45-minute sessions. Michelle watched them whizzing around the rink, spinning, jumping, and skating backward. Amazingly, they seldom ran into each other. Michelle must have thought that one day she would be that good.

Suddenly, everyone Michelle knew was a skater, a skater's mom, or a skater's coach. Day in and day out, all they talked about was skating. For the first year, Michelle and Karen went to the public school in Lake Arrowhead with the other skaters. But after that, they had private tutors.

While Michelle was basking in her sudden rise to glory, Carroll was banging his head. He quickly found out that Michelle needed a lot more work than he had originally bargained for. She was quite the rookie compared to Ice Castle's veteran skaters. She had no idea how to train with someone as experienced as Frank Carroll. Before long, she realized she had a lot of bad habits. The first thing she learned was to keep on going with her program even if she fell—just like she would do if she was competing. She had to work through her mistakes instead of giving up and starting over. Carroll taught Michelle that falling in practice was a great opportunity to learn.

Throughout 1992, while she trained with Carroll, Michelle also kept careful track of the senior skaters. It was the year Kristi Yamaguchi became the senior ladies champion, Nancy Kerrigan took silver, and Tonya Harding grabbed the bronze. Then, along with millions of people around the world, the Kwans watched Yamaguchi win gold and Kerrigan take bronze at the 1992 Winter Olympics. A few weeks later at Worlds, Yamaguchi captured another gold medal, while Kerrigan finished second. No doubt, watching those performances was inspiring for young Michelle. She must have noticed that they had a special "look" when they skated. They were beautiful young women with experience and grace. Judges liked to watch skaters who had the total package.

Meanwhile, Michelle was preparing her program for the National Junior Championships. By this time, she had already been doing a lot of triple jumps, but not consistently. Most of them were hit or miss, and that wasn't good enough for Carroll. If she was unable to hit them 80 percent of the time in practice, he would not put them in the program. Michelle's excitement gradually wore into nervousness as Nationals drew closer. One

The 1996 U.S. Figure Skating Championships was a turning point in Kwan's career. It marked the point in time when she was noticed as a woman, rather than just a young girl. After much practicing throughout the year, Kwan felt extremely comfortable with her routines, and for the first time, felt like she belonged in this competition.

had to do was listen and believe. So if she needed to become a lady, a lady she would be.

Convincing Michelle's parents was another story. In Chinese culture, a teenage girl does not wear makeup. But Carroll stressed to Danny and Estella that her look was part of the performance. He pointed out that if she was appearing in a ballet, she would have to wear stage makeup. It was no different in skating. After some coaxing, Danny and Estella agreed.

Frank Carroll, choreographer Lori Nichol, and Kwan went to work finding the right music. They finally decided on a piece called "Salome," by composer Richard Strauss. The music represented a story from the New Testament. In the story, Salome performs the dance of the seven veils for King Herod Antipas. Herod likes her dance so much that he offers her a gift of anything she wants. With her mother's advice, she asks for the head of John the Baptist on a platter. It's a seductive and gruesome story, much different from the pieces Kwan was used to performing. But she was looking for something dramatic, and this was it. Enter Salome. (Interestingly, the Bible never calls Salome by name. Playwright Oscar Wilde later gave her this name in his play *Salome*.)

Kwan and Nichol had a lot of work ahead of them. Kwan's portrayal had to be honest and convincing. She and Nichol had faith in each other. Kwan had always admired Nichol's choreography. She had a way of making a good skater look great. Up until this time, Nichol had almost sole control of the choreography. Now, she wanted Kwan to help develop it. She would have to become Salome, and the interpretation would come from inside of her.

During practices, Kwan had an emotional awakening. The music and character transformed her into an artist. Off the ice, she was the same fun-loving teenager. But once she stepped onto the ice, she became someone different. She was Salome. The program slowly took shape. Finally, the day came when she did a run-through. As the performance unfolded, Kwan's fluid movements and emotion brought tears to Nichol's eyes. Michelle beamed with satisfaction and pride.

But would it all work? Would the audience accept the new Michelle Kwan? In October 1995, she got her first chance to test her budding role at Skate America in Detroit, Michigan. Kwan was nervous. The story of Salome was pretty heavy. It was nothing like the light and bouncy programs she'd done in the past.

Perhaps people would think she was trying to act older than she really was.

She skated her short program to "Spanish Medley." "Who is that?" people whispered to each other. The perky teenager in a ponytail was gone. In her place was a striking young woman who radiated a feeling of mystery. When the music began, her transformation was obvious—the line and flow of her movements were more polished. The spectators sat back in an awed hush and soaked it all in. She ended the program with a series of breathtaking spins. Rising from a sit spin, she grabbed hold of her free leg and pulled it up, tipping her head back as she continued to spin. The artistry was spell-binding.

But the long program would hold the moment of truth. Kwan's costume was a masterpiece of glittering sequins on deep purple and flesh-colored fabrics. Her team worked almost as hard creating the costume as Kwan did on the routine, and their labor paid off. Kwan wasn't just sparkling, she was dazzling. A silver sequin pasted at the corner of each eye added a flair of seductiveness. She was ready to show the world Salome.

The program was dynamic. The Far East–flavored choreography intrigued the audience and wove all the elements together. Her presentation seemed more like a three-act play than a skating routine. The spine-tingling spiral sequences and edges were incredible to watch, even if she hadn't jumped once. When she finished, Michelle knew this was it. This person was the skater she had always dreamed of becoming. The judges agreed. She was no longer little Michelle but Miss Kwan. She finished first, ahead of Lu Chen, who had just beaten everyone to become world champion. Could Kwan and Salome do the same in 1996?

7

On Top
of the World

Each competition leading up to the 1996 Nationals brought Kwan closer to Salome. By the time she got to San Jose, California, she had skated as Salome so much that it just came natural for her. Over the year, she worked hard to polish every movement, not just the jumps and spins, so the program flowed smoothly from beginning to end.

The first three times she competed at Nationals, everyone thought of Kwan as a kid. In those days, Kwan wasn't even sure she belonged with the best skaters. Being there was like a dream come true, but she didn't feel equal to them. In 1996, it was a whole different story. Not only did she feel like she belonged, she knew if she skated her best, she would win.

Most people expected the big contest for first would be between defending champion Nicole Bobek and rising star Lady Kwan. But Bobek was nursing an ankle injury and was having some troubles with her jumps. Still, Bobek went on to skate a respectable short program. So did her new rival. Wearing a scarlet costume, Kwan's skate to "Spanish Medley" was sensational.

Michelle Kwan performs her short program at the 1996 U.S. Figure Skating Championships in San Jose, California. This performance put her in first place heading into the free skate. Her celebrated "Salome" routine earned her the U.S. Figure Skating Championship.

The "lady in red" won the short program, while Bobek clung to third.

In the warm-up before the long program, Kwan's jumps looked as sleek and powerful as those of a jungle tiger. Bobek, however, took a devastating tumble on a triple lutz. In obvious pain, she skated to the sidelines choking back tears. After conferring with her coach, Bobek decided to drop out of the competition. Kwan was slated to skate second. Oftentimes, it is a disadvantage to skate first because judges will more than likely "leave room" in the scores for the following skaters. The first skater, Sydney Vogel, left plenty of room for Kwan.

Kwan skated out onto the ice, the cherished dragon pendant from her grandmother twinkling under the lights. Once again, she was mesmerizing in her Salome makeup. She gave a magnificent performance, landing her jumps perfectly, even the treacherous triple toe–triple toe combination. Spiral by spiral, glide by glide, Kwan's movements built up to the dramatic finale—a double axel precisely timed to the music. When the moment came, she singled the jump. It didn't matter. The crowd erupted in a roar of applause and cheers. Technically, the jump was an extra, so it wouldn't result in any deductions. But Kwan knew it was supposed to be there. For a moment, she stepped out of her sophisticated presence and gave a kiddish "pow" to her head with a trigger finger.

There was no reason for Kwan to beat herself up, however. When the judges' scores came in, they had all placed her in first. It would be virtually impossible to knock her off her perch. And no one did. After all those silver medals, Kwan finally got her chance to stand on the center podium. With smiles and tears, she savored the moment. Michelle Kwan was the U.S. figure skating champion.

Even though Kwan had won Nationals, she wasn't considered the favorite to win Worlds in Edmonton, Canada. But she was one of the favorites. What's more, Nationals was not the top of the mountain. She was still building momentum.

After her short program at Worlds, Kwan again stood in first place. She knew, however, that the freeskate counted for much more, so it was really still anyone's competition to win. Going into the long program, reigning champion Lu Chen seemed as confident as ever. She delivered a gold-winning performance, even snagging two perfect 6.0s for artistic presentation. Backstage, Kwan heard the judges' scores. No woman had ever before gotten perfect scores at a World Championship. Carroll assured her that there was still enough room for her to sneak ahead.

This was her moment. As Kwan took her opening stance, she let go of herself and became Salome. Everything seemed to be going perfectly until her triple-triple toe loop combination. She did a triple-double instead. In order to make sure she had enough points to beat Lu Chen, she would have to come up with another triple. Kwan did some quick thinking. The grand finale was only seconds away. Instead of the double axel finish she had planned, Kwan decided to make it a triple toe—always a difficult jump, but especially at the end of the program when she was exhausted. Not only did she complete the jump, but it was powerful, with spring and height. It was a smashing last impression to leave with the judges.

When the scores came in, Kwan had two perfect 6.0s, too. The final tallies were tight, but she had done it. Michelle Kwan became the new world champion. Since the day she laced up her first pair of skates, Kwan had dreamed of this day. She was truly on top of the world.

LIFE AT THE TOP

The reality took a while to sink in. For a while, Kwan slept with her gold medal draped around her neck. It was an exciting time in her life. Suddenly, she was getting hundreds of calls for interviews and appearances. She even got invited to visit President Bill Clinton at the White House. Although she would have loved to go, she had to turn him down. She just didn't have time. Giving interview after interview, she

OFF THE ICE

With all the talk about skating, training, and competitions, it is easy to forget that Kwan was still a regular kid. Although she had a crazy schedule, she had a life outside the rink. One of her favorite pastimes was and still is shopping for clothes, makeup, and music. She has lots of favorite musicians, including Natalie Merchant, Tracy Chapman, Jewel, and Celine Dion. Up until she was 13, she wore only hand-me-down clothes. When she could finally afford to buy new clothes, she took it seriously. She's still a bargain hunter, however.

On days off, she likes to go to the movies with her friends, especially if an action-adventure film is playing at the theater. Her favorite movie stars include Brad Pitt, Harrison Ford, Leonardo DiCaprio, and Jim Carrey. Of course, she's seen the few skating movies there are at least dozens of times. One of them is a film from the 1970s called *Ice Castles,* about a girl who keeps skating even after she goes blind. More recently, *The Cutting Edge* is about a snotty girl who becomes a pairs partner with a hockey player.

Like most kids, Kwan loved amusement parks like Six Flags Magic Mountain and Disneyland; her favorite ride is the Colossus at Magic Mountain. One of her favorite adventures was a whitewater rafting trip she took with some skaters while on tour in 1995. While she was on the raft, she was so scared that she wished it would be over. Then when it ended, she wanted to do it all over again.

Once she turned 16, Kwan, like most teenagers, was eager to get her driver's license. But she flunked her first test. A few weeks later, she took it again with a different examiner and passed.

After she won 1996 Worlds, many people on the street started to recognize Kwan and ask for her autograph. That treatment was hard for her to get used to.

Like many young people, Kwan also keeps a diary. In fact, she calls it her best buddy and writes everything in it. She's not very good at hiding the little book, however. From time to time, it pops up in strange places, like the middle of the kitchen table. Since the diary is very small she has to use tiny handwriting, so she doesn't think anyone could read it anyway.

On the ice, she is a figure skating master, untouchable by most, but off the ice she's a regular person. She has somehow always managed to keep her attitude humble and down to earth.

had to learn how to tell the same story over and over again as if she had never told it before. Being an open and chatty young lady, Kwan sometimes found herself rattling off answers to questions without thinking it through. "Sometimes I'd rewind what I had said and think, 'That was so stupid!'" she admitted in *Heart of a Champion*. "But it was too late to change it."

She also joined a 50-city tour in which she got paid a reported $750,000. But her agent, Shep Goldberg, wouldn't let the money go to her head. She had to be selective about her appearances and think about her future. In fact, she turned down 75 percent of the requests she got. Touring the country from coast to coast, Kwan skated with her whole heart and soul, and the audiences loved her. The skating firecracker had quickly become America's little sweetheart.

Yes, Kwan had emerged on the skating circuit as the world champ. But she was still working hard to improve herself, especially her triple axel. She wanted to get every element perfected before the 1998 Olympics in Nagano, Japan. Going into 1996–1997, 16-year-old Kwan wondered how in the world she could ever top Salome. Would she be able to find a program equally dramatic and inspiring?

For her new short program, Kwan skated to William Shakespeare's tragedy *Othello*. She would take the role of Desdemona, the gentle wife of the Moorish general Othello. In the play, Othello is tricked into believing that his wife has cheated on him. Furious with jealousy, he murders Desdemona, despite her pleas of innocence. Othello eventually finds out the truth. In anguish, he then kills himself.

When developing the freeskate, Kwan dug into the history of India's famous Taj Mahal, one of the Seven Wonders of the World. The marble tomb stands in a beautiful garden surrounded by pools of water that reflect its glory. Over the years, millions of people have gazed in awe at the monument but few know about its intriguing past. More than 300 years ago, ruler Shah Jahan ordered the magnificent tomb to be built in memory of his favorite wife, Mumtaz-i-Mahal, which means "pride of the palace." The romantic love Shah Jahan had for his wife inspired many love stories. In her long program, Kwan would portray Mumtaz-i-Mahal.

After winning the world title, Kwan faced intense pressure to keep going. Once a competitor reaches the top, she doesn't want to think about losing. Kwan took some time off from exhibitions to work on her new routines. Things were going well, but she was having trouble breaking in her new boots. She had signed an endorsement contract with Riedell, a manufacturer of ice skates, and had to wear their boots.

In November, she traveled to Paris for the Trophée Lalique. Desdemona turned out to be a masterpiece, and Kwan won the short program hands down. In the long program, she had a few problems with her double axel and triple flip—her boots were bothering her—but she didn't even stumble. Feeling the jumps weren't quite right, she "tilted" in the air to rescue the jumps and land correctly. Skaters who can save jumps this way are said to have "cat feet." Kwan was definitely one of those skaters. Her final spin sequence was a knockout, and she won the event. Fourteen-year-old up-and-comer Tara Lipinski finished third.

For now, it seemed like the queen would continue her reign. Even Carroll believed Kwan would rocket through the season with flying colors. But one thought continued to haunt Kwan. She knew she couldn't be a world champion forever.

CLIPPED WINGS

The media had built Kwan into a superhero on ice. Eventually, something would have to give. "I'm not an alien or a super-duper jumping machine who lands on her feet all the time," Kwan said, according to Edward Z. Epstein's *Born to Skate*. "I'm normal!" The 1997 U.S. Nationals were held in Nashville, Tennessee, the home of country music. All of the best skaters gathered there with the same goal, to knock Kwan off her throne. Carroll understood that Kwan was experiencing something new this year. Her emotions ranged from apprehensive to terrified.

But Kwan was in an unfocused state of mind. It was a tremendous amount of pressure for a 16-year-old to handle. In practice, she was suddenly having big troubles with her jumps. To make matters worse, she was slated to skate second in the short program. Kwan was used to skating toward the end of the evening, when the judges and audiences were settled in and anticipation was heightened. Performing at the top of the evening was just one more uncomfortable twinge in a painful competition.

Nevertheless, Kwan managed to get through the short program and was in first place. Tara Lipinski was nipping at her heels. On the night of the long program, Kwan looked focused as she stood at the edge of the rink talking to Carroll. She was radiant in a glittering red and gold costume, every inch the princess she was portraying. Opening with exquisite choreography, she hushed the crowd. After a flying camel spin, she went into her triple lutz–double toe combination. She landed it. Next, she moved into the triple-triple toe loop combination. Failing to come out of the jump forcefully enough, she fell hard and toppled onto her stomach. The crowd was shocked. After the fall, Kwan panicked. In her next jump, the triple flip, she bobbled her landing. She managed a textbook double axel, followed by some intricate footwork. But she aborted her second triple lutz and made it a double.

Undoubtedly, the spectators wondered what was happening to Michelle Kwan, skating superstar. "I wasn't concentrating enough," Kwan later said, according to *Born to Skate*. "I guess I panicked in the middle of the performance after that fall. I got scared." But the program wasn't over. She delivered a blockbuster triple salchow and a high-flying triple toe loop. The crowd admired her perseverance and gave her an ovation. She pressed her palms to her cheeks in embarrassment but bravely threw a kiss to the audience and waved. Kwan had always compared her skating to flying. Suddenly, it seemed like someone had clipped her wings. Her marks were high enough to keep her in first, but only with a razor-thin lead over Tara Lipinski.

Lipinski was next in the lineup. All she had to do was skate a flawless program and she could be the next U.S. champion. She performed her technical elements with incredible precision. Her jumps were neat, clean, and complete. Once she had finished the required elements, she knew the title was most likely hers. But she didn't stop there. She continued with a daring second triple lutz, a double axel–triple salchow combination, and a final triple toe. The audience jumped to their feet, chanting, "Six! Six! Six!" She had won. Kwan had been bumped to second.

Later, Kwan met with the media. Undoubtedly, she was frustrated and disappointed. Perhaps she was a bit resentful toward her young contender for doing just what she had wanted to do. If she was, she didn't show it. Kwan gracefully accepted her

Michelle Kwan takes a fall during her free skate routine at the 1997 U.S. Figure Skating Championships in Nashville, Tennessee. At a press conference in 1998, her coach Frank Carroll said, "Every athlete that exists falls on a daily basis at every practice session," he said. "If they are not falling, they are not working hard."

defeat and even thanked her fans for standing by her and applauding in the middle of the program.

Many thoughts charged through Kwan's brain after her defeat. She replayed her mistakes over and over again. But what really ate at her was that she let fear sneak into her psyche. At the same time, she was glad she didn't win. It wouldn't have felt fair if she hadn't skated her best and still won.

Frank Carroll was just thankful this wasn't an Olympic year. He knew Kwan was engaged in a battle with herself. She'd just have to fight it out. On the other hand, Kwan was determined to do better at the Worlds. Hopefully, she would square the whole ordeal with herself before the World Championships in March.

In 1997, the World Championships took Kwan to Switzerland. Lausanne—less than a mile from Lake Geneva—is located high up in the snow-capped Alps. Dotted with lush green valleys and turquoise lakes, the scene seemed like something out of a fairy tale. Kwan hoped this story would have a happy ending.

In the short program, Tara Lipinski skated before Kwan. Her routine was solid, quick, and powerful. Although her scores put her in first, they were certainly beatable. Kwan took the ice wearing a sophisticated black costume. She appeared confident and focused. When "Dreams of Desdemona" began, Kwan's body flowed like silk in a breeze; her spirals were breathtaking. Going into her triple lutz–double toe loop combination, she built up great speed, but she waited a little too long to take the tap and over-rotated. She fell out of the jump and took a forbidden extra step before tackling the double toe loop, resulting in a major deduction. The rest of the program was exquisite, but it wasn't enough. After the short, Kwan stood in a fourth. Her rival Tara Lipinski sat in first.

Again, Lipinski skated before Kwan in the freeskate. And once again, she had a solid performance. Rinkside with Carroll, Kwan's expression was serious and determined. As soon as Kwan's program started, she soared. She didn't just skate, she acted out the part of the Indian princess. Everything finally fell into place, and she gave a knockout performance. At the end of the night, Kwan had catapulted from fourth to silver, losing her world title to Lipinski. Lipinski also broke Kwan's record of being the youngest world champion.

Although she hadn't come out with the gold, Kwan had won a personal triumph. She conquered the battle within herself. It had been a rough year for Kwan but it ended in glory. Back on track, she could focus on 1998—the year of the Olympics.

8

Back in Action

After the Worlds, once again Kwan performed in the Campbell's Soups Tour of World Figure Skating Champions. In 1996, she would earn more than $1 million. Also, she took first place in the Hershey's Kisses Skating Challenge, bringing down several perfect 6.0s. It looked as though Kwan was bouncing back. In July, she teamed up with Olympic champion Brian Boitano for Skating Romance III in Atlantic City, New Jersey. The two had become close friends on the Campbell's Soups Tour. One of Kwan's first skating heroes, Boitano personally chose her as his costar.

Going into the 1997–1998 season, Kwan's objective was to keep the confidence level high and learn from her mistakes. "This year I put a lot of pressure on myself," she said about 1997 in Chip Lovitt's *Skating for the Gold: Michelle Kwan and Tara Lipinski*. "I got focused on the wrong thing, and I learned my lesson." After her Nashville program, Kwan said she skated like a chicken with her head chopped off. She now believed she got things back together.

During the winter of 1997, Kwan was going through all sorts of changes, emotionally and physically. She was growing, gaining weight, and budding into a young woman. When weight distribution shifts on a young skater, it takes a little adjusting to regain the balance. Also, Kwan still wasn't pleased with her boots. One day for practice, she slipped on a pair of SP-Teris instead of the Riedells. The switch made all the difference in the world. With two years left on the contract, the Riedell boots were history. Even though the Kwans hated to go back on their word, they really had no choice. When choosing between an endorsement or a potential Olympic medal, the decision was a no-brainer.

Kwan was ready to attack a new season. Her first stop was Skate America in Detroit, Michigan. In Detroit's Joe Louis Arena, skaters warmed up for the short program. The competition was sure to be a smash, with Kwan and Tara Lipinski dueling it out again and about to unveil their new programs. This night would mark the beginning of the Olympic season and would set the tone for the coming events. A lot was riding on this six-minute warm-up.

On the ice, Lipinski shined with confidence. Over the summer, she had grown just an inch or so and gained a measly six pounds, which had spread themselves out evenly. She still had the perfect jumping body.

On the other hand, Kwan was wobbling on her jumps. She barely rescued her first attempt at a triple lutz. She tried another, but she had to put her hand down on the ice to keep from falling. A few moments later, she stumbled on her feet. Finally she slipped and fell while doing a double axel. Getting up, she skated a few steps then slid to a stop in the center of the rink, put her hands on her hips, and stared up into the lights. Questions must have raced through her mind. What is going on? Could the horror possibly be happening again? She shook her head free of the thoughts. It's only warm-up. Carroll reassured her. Then they discussed the troubles she had on each jump.

Shortly, Kwan was back on the ice, this time for real. Dressed in a sleeveless red-and-cream-colored dress, she took a deep breath and waited for her music to start. She would skate to *Lyra Angelica*, or *Angel's Song*, a concerto for harp and string orchestra. There was no kidding anyone, the pressure on Kwan was intense. Her performance that night would give her the confidence she needed going forward. Twenty-seven seconds into her program, she flew into that pesky triple lutz, this time on her trusty SP-Teri skates. She came down solidly, straight and tall, and followed with a smooth double toe loop. Effortlessly, she glided through the rest of her program. She had done it—skated a clean short program. Her technical marks were solid, 5.7s and 5.8s. Then came the marks for presentation, all 5.9s. Michelle Kwan was back in action.

Next, Lipinski moved onto the ice. She skated to music from the children's animated film *Anastasia*. As usual, she performed the most difficult jumps. She bobbled a bit on her combination spin near the end, but otherwise, she delivered a solid performance. Even though Lipinski had tougher jumps than Kwan, her scores came in lower. The artistic marks also drooped in comparison. Lipinski seemed puzzled by the numbers. How could the judges rank the jumping genius so low? Like Kwan, she had to learn that there was more to figure skating than athletics. Judges not only wanted someone who could jump, they wanted an elegant skater as well.

Even the reporters were perplexed at the scores of the reigning champ. But Carroll helped set things straight. He explained that Kwan's footwork and spiral sequence were just as difficult as the triple lutz–triple toe loop. "We seem to be sidetracked and thinking only jumping is difficult," he said, according to Christine Brennan's *Edge of Glory*. "I don't think there's a girl in the world who could do that spiral sequence except Michelle." The judges obviously agreed with him.

The next evening, the skaters returned for the long program. Once again, Kwan skated before Lipinski. Before she skated out onto the ice, Carroll told her to let herself go and have fun. Fun—it was a word Kwan had lost during her disastrous season. Maybe now was the time to test it out again. Throughout her program, Kwan's footwork, fancy spins, and elegant spirals brought applause after applause. At one point, she spiraled in one direction then switched back in the other direction. No one else in the world had ever tried it. It would be like trying to write with the wrong hand. She wobbled slightly, but her bold attempt of the stunt would rank up there with a triple jump. Of course, she did plenty of jumps, too. She landed seven triples, including two tricky triple lutzes. The scores were impressive, all 5.8s for technical merit and all 5.9s for presentation.

Still, not everyone loved her long program. Some people thought it lacked the emotion of her previous dramatic roles. But Kwan knew exactly what she was doing. "When I'm eighty years old and I'm looking back, I don't want to see Salome or any character, I want to see me," she said in *Edge of Glory*. Another dissatisfied customer was her choreographer, Lori Nichol. In her opinion, there were things that needed tweaking. It wasn't Kwan's fault, but Nichol wanted to make sure the choreography was stunning and worthy of Kwan's talent.

Back on the ice, Lipinski held her breath. She needed an amazing skate to beat Kwan, and she would try. Perhaps, she tried too hard. Eighty seconds in, on her triple lutz, she crashed down on the ice. Near the end of her program, she got tangled up in a sequence of triple jumps and finished the program three seconds too late. She would have to settle for second place—the gold belonged to Kwan, who was back again, having fun and loving to skate.

A CAST FOR KWAN

In November, Kwan went to Skate Canada in Halifax, Nova Scotia. She won the short program with seven 5.9s and the freeskate and title with three more 5.9s. After her poor skating in the long program, it was amazing Kwan got any 5.9s. She doubled two

Fellow skater Michael Chack signs Michelle Kwan's cast at the Ice Castle International Training Center in Lake Arrowhead, California, in 1997.
A few months later, in January 1998, Kwan won a U.S. Figure Skating Championship, stress fracture and all.

triples and fell on her final move, a flying butterfly, which she later dubbed "a dead butterfly," according to *Edge of Glory*.

Originally, Kwan was not slated to skate in Canada. Her two championship series events were Skate America and the NHK Trophy on Olympic Ice in Japan. But top skaters are allowed to enter a third for extra experience and prize money. Danny Kwan wanted her to go. Reportedly, she received an appearance fee of as much as $100,000.

Dead set against it, Carroll refused to go with her. She didn't have to do it, and she was nursing a sore foot. In August 1996, she suffered a stress fracture in the second toe of her left foot. (Interestingly, the Kwans never released a statement about the original injury, so this was the first time anyone was hearing about it.) Carroll figured why push it.

Sure enough, Kwan reinjured the foot during Skate Canada. Apparently, it was the reason she slipped and fell on the butterfly spin at the end of the long program. The cast went on November 15 and came off November 26, the day before Thanksgiving. Because of the injury, Kwan missed the NHK Trophy and the champions series final in Munich. But that was okay with Carroll. All he cared about were Nationals and the Olympics.

All fears about Kwan's injury were put to rest at the 1998 U.S. Championships. Kwan rocked the house with her history-making perfect scores. With Lipinski's shaky last few performances, all eyes were on Kwan to win Olympic gold.

A CLOSE SECOND

In the months building up to the Olympics, it seemed like Kwan and Tara Lipinski were rivals on and off the ice, even though Kwan claimed they were friends off the ice and competitors on it. Both had published autobiographies. Just like on the ice, Kwan's *Heart of a Champion* was more thoughtful and introspective than Lipinski's *Triumph on Ice*. Even their school grades faced off. In September, Shep Goldberg sent out a press release: "The first marks of the season are in and with scores ranging from 3.5 to 4.0 you would think Michelle Kwan would be unhappy. On the contrary. The seventeen-year-old skating champion is thrilled because the marks refer not to her skating prowess but to her high school grades." When reporters asked Tara's agent, Mike Burg, if he was going to respond with his own press release on Lipinski's grades, he laughed and said no. He had already invited the press to witness her being tutored. That was good enough.

Regardless of who got better grades, one thing was for sure—both girls wanted the gold. For Kwan, this was the moment she had been waiting for ever since she first stepped on the ice. But skating can be unpredictable. Oftentimes, a medal is only about who skates better on a particular day. What if she didn't win? "I guess I'll be disappointed," Kwan admitted, according to Lovitt's *Skating for the Gold*. "But you have to learn to cope and be happy and enjoy life. A lot of things aren't going to go your way."

Missing the opening ceremonies, Kwan came to the Olympic Games in Nagano, Japan, a little late. Her competition didn't come until near the end of the Games, so she opted to stay home and get some last-minute treatment for her toe. Also, she wanted to keep things as normal as possible. She wanted to treat this competition the same as all the others. She didn't want to get too psyched out about it. Once she arrived, she even chose not to stay in the Olympic Village. She was only one of two of the nearly 200 U.S. athletes who did not. (Nicole Bobek was the other.) Instead, she wanted to bunk up with her parents, just as she did at Nationals or Worlds.

Just before noon on Tuesday, February 10, Kwan got ready to start her first Olympic practice. With cameras poised, the media began recording the big event. CBS Sports ran it live on television back in America. Wearing a black practice outfit, Kwan began skating to *Lyra Angelica*. She didn't expect too much from the practice. Only in Nagano for 10 hours, she was jet-lagged and exhausted. As always, she began with her triple lutz, and she fell. The 50 journalists huddled by the sideboards took note. Kwan, the Olympic gold medal favorite, crashed on her first official jump at the Games.

Like in any other practice, Kwan just kept going. She landed one triple jump after another. In fact, she nailed down everything else in her program—the six other triples and her double axel. If she was feeling the pressure, it didn't show. She looked calm and happy.

Finally, the night of the short program arrived. This was sure to be Kwan's finest hour. All those years of lessons and competitions and medals had been building up to this one moment in time. Kwan skated out into the center of White Ring arena. The music began. One by one, the elements blended together, every triple, every spiral. Kwan was swept up in the magic. As the music intensified, she circled in to her mesmerizing spiral in which she raised her left leg high and spun on the blade of her right skate. She spun to a finish and soaked in the applause. She had been flawless, just like she had always dreamed she would. At the end of the night, Kwan was in first, Lipinski a close second. Kwan could almost feel the gold medal in her hands, but there was no mistake, Lipinski was still within striking distance.

Later on, Kwan and Lipinski drew their skating positions for the long program on Friday night. Kwan drew a harsh first, Lipinski fifth. Still, Kwan was okay with the lineup. It would cut into her warm-up time, shaving off about two minutes. But she could stay in her skates and get right back out on the ice. On the other hand, judges always leave room in the first skater's scores for the following skaters. No matter how exquisitely Kwan skated, there would be no 6.0s; she could probably only expect 5.8s and 5.9s. Any higher score would prejudge the competition. Although it may seem unfair, it's the way the system works. And Kwan knew the rules. It was just the luck of the draw.

Even though her program was wonderful, Carroll thought Kwan was holding back. Understandably, Kwan didn't want to take chances. After all, this was the Olympics. Carroll hoped she would skate her long program with more energy and really let herself go free.

At 9:30 on Friday night, Kwan stepped out from behind the blue backstage curtains. Her Olympic moment was waiting for her. On the ice, she didn't smile. She was focused on what he had to do. Slowly, cautiously, she began to skate. She knew the music; she knew the moves. Seventy-five seconds into the program, she hung on to a triple flip. Eleven seconds later, she came out of a double axel. She flowed with the music. Her second triple lutz was stronger and higher than her first, certainly gold medal material. All her jumps behind her, Kwan moved back toward the center of the ice. She was just slightly behind her music, so her wing-it, "Olympic moment" move was a second too late. But it still was a spine-tingling performance. She clung to Carroll in Kiss and Cry. In Kwan's mind, it couldn't have gone better.

The first set of marks popped up: 5.7s and 5.8s. Moments later, the presentation marks showed all 5.9s, as wonderful as ever. Those 5.7s were beatable, however. Kwan's gold medal dream was skating on thin ice.

Finally, Tara Lipinski stepped into the rink. She fired through her program with energy and life. Her triples were all show-stoppers. When the music ended, she could hardly contain herself. She breathlessly started running across the ice toward her coach. Less than a minute later, in Kiss and Cry, she got her scores. 5.9s and 5.8s for technical merit. And for presentation, six judges out of nine put her in first place. She had defeated the favorite. Kwan would take silver. At 15, Tara Lipinski became the youngest Olympic figure skating champion ever.

Most people would agree that Kwan was a much more polished, artistic, and passionate skater. She had skated superbly enough to win any other Olympics. But on that particular night, the judges thought differently. Upon hearing the news, Kwan burst into tears.

Soon, Lipinski climbed the medals podium. Kwan stood below and behind her, eyes red and makeup gone from crying. She graciously bowed her head to receive her silver medal. The two skaters watched the U.S. flags glide up the poles. Lipinski was giddy with delight. Kwan seemed dazed, but composed.

At the press conference later that night, Kwan proved her elegance extended beyond the ice. "I knew this competition wasn't going to be a piece of cake," she said. "I came here looking for a good performance, and I skated my best. . . . This might not be the color medal that I wanted but I'll take it." In a moment that would test the strongest will, Kwan remained a class act. "I'm happy," she said. "You never know what you are going to get."

Then, the reporters asked the inevitable. What about the rivalry? Lipinski went first and talked about what a fabulous night it was. She added that Kwan had skated great, even though she had not watched. Next, it was Kwan's turn. She took the microphone in her hand and looked right into Lipinski's eyes. "I like you, Tara," she spoke sincerely.

The comment took dozens of reporters by surprise, and it left Lipinski speechless. In this moment, Kwan displayed grace beyond her years. She understood why Lipinski had won—she could jump, tear across the ice, and remind everyone what it was like to be 15. Lipinski may not have had the total package, but Kwan respected her performance.

After Nagano, Kwan's first thoughts were of the World Championships the following month in Minneapolis, Minnesota. Perhaps she would be able to capture the gold there. For Lipinski, the Worlds would turn out to be greater pressure than the Olympics. If Kwan beat her, would everyone think her Olympic gold was a fluke? Kwan easily won gold for the second year in a row, despite a fall on her double axel in the long program. The following summer, Kwan skated with Lipinski on the Champions on Ice tour. When Kwan stepped out on the ice, she got a much warmer welcome than Lipinski. Post-Olympic endorsements also favored Kwan over Lipinski. She got offers from Caress soap and four prime-time ABC-Disney television specials, the first of which was based on the Disney animated

Silver medalist Michelle Kwan *(left)*, gold medalist Tara Lipinski *(center)*, and bronze medalist Lu Chen stand during the United States' national anthem at the 1998 Winter Olympics in Nagano, Japan. At age 17, Kwan finished in second place, losing to fellow American Lipinski by a tenth of a point.

movie *Mulan.* As it turned out, silver was doing better than gold. To America, Kwan was still the champion and her sportsman-like attitude set her skyscrapers above the rest.

Kwan's Olympic dream hadn't come true—yet. She wasn't about to give up. "I have my chance in 2002," she said, according to *Edge of Glory.* "If I want it bad enough, I'm going to go and try again."

9

Post-Olympic Glow

On a warm afternoon in late April, the 1998 Olympians gathered on the South Lawn of the White House. A soft breeze brushed across Kwan's face as she squinted toward the lectern where President Bill Clinton stood. Out of the 200 athletes in front of him, Clinton singled out one member of the U.S. figure skating team. "I would like to introduce the athlete who has been chosen by her teammates to represent the Olympians here today," President Clinton said, "a person whose grace and excellence on the ice, and I must say, even more after the competition, must have been a source of enormous joy and pride, not only to her teammates, but to all Americans." He was, of course, referring to Michelle Kwan.

Kwan, who was standing beside Tara Lipinski, took several steps forward to the microphone and held up a U.S. Olympic Team jacket. "President Clinton, on behalf of all the athletes, coaches, trainers, and officials who represented the United States at Nagano," she said, "we'd like to show our thanks for all your support and present this team jacket to you, to make you

President Bill Clinton and silver medalist Michelle Kwan (right) pose on the South Lawn of the White House in Washington, D.C. Clinton hosted a ceremony honoring the 1998 Paralympic and Olympic teams, where Kwan presented the president with a U.S. Olympic team jacket.

an honorary member of the 1998 U.S. Winter Olympic Team." She handed the jacket to President Clinton, and the band struck up a bouncy tune.

The Lipinski camp, especially Tara's coach and parents, were outraged by the ceremony. They thought Lipinski's triumph had been ignored. Why should the silver medalist get to be the guest of honor? But to the U.S. Olympic Committee (USOC), the choice was obvious. Over the years, Kwan had exhibited the spirit of a true champion—humble in victory, gracious in defeat. Her presence on the Olympic team was a tremendous compliment to American athletes. On the other hand, the Lipinski team became known for grumbling sportsmanship and poor manners. For the USOC, it was an open-shut decision. Kwan would be the team representative.

There was yet another reason the USOC chose Kwan. She had already made it pretty clear that she planned to go on to the 2002 Winter Olympics in Salt Lake City, Utah. Lipinski was a bit wishy-washy on the subject, and it seemed unlikely she would be competing.

However, the sting of defeat took awhile to heal. When dreams crash, there is always some pain. After she got back home from Nagano, Kwan and Danny sat down and looked over the short list of Olympic figure skating gold medalists. They counted how many Olympic champions there have been, and it twisted Kwan's heart that she wasn't one of them.

She wasn't the first American silver medalist to come home bitterly disappointed. She followed skating superstars like Frank Carroll's former student Linda Fratianne and skating legend Janet Lynn. And in the 1994 Olympics, Kwan watched Nancy Kerrigan get bumped out of gold as well. Still, when she looked at her silver medal, she felt proud, unlike Fratianne, who competed in the 1980 Olympics. Fratianne felt so let down after losing gold that it took her 15 years to open the box holding her silver medal and look at it.

In late July and August, Kwan competed at the Goodwill Games on Long Island, New York. The night of the women's competition, 10,000 people packed into Nassau Coliseum. This Olympic-style competition would be the last time she would skate to *Lyra Angelica*. It would be a fond, but sad, parting. For the ninth time, she skated her short program to Rachmaninoff, and for the ninth time she did it without a mistake. Again, her scores were untouchable—one 6.0 and the rest 5.9s. In the long program, she fell on a triple loop and doubled a triple salchow, but first place still belonged to her. When she finished, it was almost as if the audience was giving her a big group hug. She basked in the post-Olympic glow. She wasn't the Olympic champion, but it didn't matter. She was more popular than ever, and Kwan finally realized why. It was that silver medal.

Kwan learned that sometimes the victory wasn't as important as how a competitor handles defeat. "As people teach their children about competition, about the ups and downs and how to deal with them, I guess I can stand as a model," she said in her last press conference of the Olympic season. "They can say, 'She didn't win, but she's still standing up tall and smiling and loving the sport.' "

DON'T COUNT HER OUT

Four years is a long time. Why would Kwan put herself through another four years of rigorous training and competitive skating for one more shot at Olympic gold? For Kwan, the answer was simple. "I love competing," she said, according to Christine Brennan's *Edge of Glory*. "I love the challenge."

In 1999, Kwan enrolled at the University of California, Los Angeles (UCLA). During her freshman year, she had a lot of trouble balancing her schoolwork and skating. Before she started college, she usually practiced three times a day. In the fall of 1999, she cut back to once a day. "I want to do something other than just skate," she told Russell Scott Smith in *Sports Illustrated Women*. "It's hard to think of skating a hundred percent of the time." Although Carroll and Nichol didn't want to discourage her from going to school, her drop in commitment was frustrating to them. "We were ready to take her further," Nichol commented in the *Sports Illustrated Women* article. "And she had less time for skating than ever before." Her lack of focus showed in her skating, and she struggled through most of the season.

Kwan's programs looked pretty stagnant in the 1999 and 2000 seasons compared to one of her longtime rivals, Russian skater Irina Slutskaya. During this time, Slutskaya was perfecting complicated combinations such as a triple salchow–triple loop. Kwan rarely attempted triple-triple jumps and got the rap from some judges who thought she wasn't pushing her technical abilities. She still managed to take first in the U.S. Championships, but the 1999 Worlds would be another story. She lost the world title to another Russian competitor, Maria Butyrskaya. During the 2000 season, many people began to count Kwan out, saying she was no longer competitive.

But once again, Kwan's slump would be short-lived. In 2000, she won her fourth National Championship. She then went on to beat the odds and win the 2000 World Championships, making her the first skater to reclaim the world title twice in a career. People learned never to underestimate Michelle Kwan again. After a rocky start, the four-year trek between Olympics started to roll right along for Kwan. In 2001, she captured her fourth consecutive, and fifth overall, national title.

In March 2001, she was off to Vancouver, Canada, to defend her world title. Once again, she faced off with Slutskaya. At the Worlds, Slutskaya became the first woman to complete a triple-triple-double combination. During the 2000–2001 season, Slutskaya had already beaten Kwan in two head-to-head skates—Skate Canada and the Grand Prix Final. Slutskaya thought this might be her year to take down Kwan and win the World Championships.

At the 2001 Worlds, Kwan skated her short program to music from the classic movie *East of Eden*. She floated across the ice to the music with smooth exits from her triple flip and double axel. She two-footed the landing on her triple lutz–double toe loop combination. But her superb spiral sequences and footwork—the most difficult in the competition—were enough to awe the judges. When she did a split jump during her footwork, the crowd roared wildly. Unable to stay seated any longer, the audience jumped to a standing ovation while she was still swirling in her final spiral.

Despite Kwan's dramatic performance, Slutskaya won the short program, leaving Kwan in second. As always, Slutskaya's jumps were untouchable, and her spins were fast and well-centered. However, her presentation was not as strong or memorable as Kwan's.

Kwan and Slutskaya were not the only contenders at the 2001 World Championships. Fifteen-year-old American Sarah Hughes muscled her jumps and skated with incredible ease and expression. She sat in fourth place at the end of the short program. American Angela Nikodinov had the skate of her life at the short program. She powered through her program with genuine expression and a gracefulness that could almost match Kwan's. Her one-of-a-kind layback spin was untouchable. At the end of the night, she finished an amazing third.

On the night of the long program, the top skaters tried to hang onto their spots or climb up to one better. Nikodinov skated like a ballerina. At one lovely moment, she blew a kiss to the crowd. But she missed two crucial jumps and fell to fifth. Sarah Hughes powered through her program with great speed and impressive footwork and spirals that pulsed to the music. She landed two triple lutzes and grabbed a triple salchow–triple loop combination. Like Kwan in her early days, Hughes seemed to lack the maturity and presence of an experienced skater. Still, she moved up to bronze.

Kwan and Slutskaya were left to fight for gold. Skating to "Song of the Black Swan," Kwan delivered a flawlessly smooth program. One element flowed into the next, looking easy, soft, and light. In her jumps, Kwan seemed to almost float up into the air and gracefully drift back down to the ice. She flew through two triple lutzes and a triple-triple toe loop combination. It was a solid gold skate, but would she have the medal to match? Compared to Kwan, Slutskaya's program looked sloppy. Her jumps were higher, but not as smooth. Her presentation was bubbly and full of smiles, but she just didn't have the artistry to beat Kwan. The world title was Kwan's to keep, and Slutskaya settled for silver.

Winning gold again, Kwan became the first four-time American world champion since 1960. After Worlds, everyone expected these two epic skaters to battle it out again for the gold medal at the Salt Lake Olympics the next year.

In the 2001–2002 season leading up to the Olympics, Kwan kept roaring like a freight train. For many, it was no surprise when she won her sixth U.S. Championship. Kwan had waited four long years for a second chance at Olympic gold. Certainly she felt this time she would stand on the center podium, earning her spot on the list of Olympic champions. Undoubtedly, the skating world thought she deserved it.

TWO HUGE SPOTS

Before the 2000–2001 season, few people paid much attention to 15-year-old Sarah Hughes. But she quickly earned a reputation for technical pizzazz, including her triple salchow–triple loop combinations. Rumor had it she was also working on an extremely rare triple loop–triple loop. Her technical prowess landed her podium spots in all three of her Grand Prix events, second at the U.S. Nationals, and a bronze at Worlds in Vancouver. She was having her dream season, with no inkling to where it might end up.

On the other hand, Kwan's Olympic season started out in upheaval. In June 2001, she fired Lori Nichols after working with her for nearly eight years, and hired Sarah Kawahara, who had choreographed her past three TV specials. The switch seemed risky, especially so close to the Olympics. "When you change choreographers it changes your flow," said former gold medalist Peggy Fleming in *Sports Illustrated Women*. "I don't know if I would do it." In September, Kwan debuted her new program—set to music from Rimsky-Korsakov's *Scheherazade*—at the Goodwill Games in Brisbane, Australia. She flubbed two jumps and seemed distracted and almost unhappy. She finished second to top Olympic rival Slutskaya. A month later, she again lost to the 22-year-old Russian skater at the Masters of Figure Skating Competition in San Diego, California.

After these two shaky performances, Carroll came up with 10 suggestions on how to spark up her training. When he gave them to Kwan, she said she wanted to practice alone for a couple of

FIGURE SKATING SCORES–THE NEW MATH

The International Skating Union (ISU) is the governing body for international competitions. The ISU oversees the World Championships and figure skating events at the Winter Olympic Games. Prior to 2004, skating was judged for technical merit in the freeskate, required elements in the short, and presentation in both programs. The marks ranged from 0.0 to 6.0 and were used to determine a preference ranking for each judge. The highest mark a judge gave to a particular skater put that skater in first place from that particular judge. At the end of the long program, the placements, 1, 2, 3, and so on, for both programs were added together. The skater with the lowest score ended up the winner.

During the 2002 Olympic Games, there was a judging scandal in the pairs event. The Russian skaters won the short program over the Canadian pair. In the final program, the Russian pair stumbled during their double axel, while the Canadians skated a flawless program. The results were a 5–4 split in favor of the Russians. Judges from Russia, China, Poland, Ukraine, and France put the Russian skaters in first place. Judges from the United States, Canada, Germany, and Japan chose the Canadians. When confronted after the event, the French judge confessed that she had been pressured by the head of the French skating organization to vote for the Russian pair. Apparently, it was part of a deal to get an advantage for the French couple who would be skating in the ice dancing competition a few days later. After this, the ISU decided to come up with a new judging system to avoid such controversies.

The New Judging System (NJS) or Code of Points is a bit more confusing than the old system, but it is also believed to be more fair. Under the new system, judges individually award technical marks for each skating element. First, each element is judged by a technical specialist who identifies the specific element. The specialist uses instant replay to judge pieces of the element, such as the exact foot position at takeoff and landing of a jump. Then, the specialist assigns a base value to the element. A panel of twelve judges awards a mark for how well the skater executed the move, an integer between -3 to +3. The value is averaged by randomly selecting 9 of the 12 judges' scores. This average is then added to or subtracted from the base value to get the actual mark for the element.

At the senior level, the short program has 8 elements to judge, and the long has 13. The base value for jumps is as follows: quad toe loop (9), triple axel (7.5), triple lutz (6), triple flip (5.5), triple loop (5), triple salchow (4.5), triple toe loop (4), and double axel (3.3). Combination jumps are marked as a single element with a base mark equal to the sum of the base marks for the individual jumps. For example, a triple flip–triple loop combination would have a base mark of 10.5.

The former presentation mark has been replaced by five categories, called program components—skating skills, transitions, performance, choreography, and interpretation. The judges award each component a raw mark on a scale of 1 to 10, with a mark of 5 being "average." The five raw marks are then combined into a program mark by multiplying them by a factor for the program and the level. For senior ladies, the factor is 0.8 for the short program and 1.6 for the long program. The new scoring system was used at the 2006 Winter Olympic Games. It will take a while for everyone to get used to the new system, but it is hoped that the new system will prevent another judging scandal like the one at Salt Lake City.

days. "Fine," Carroll said, according to *Sports Illustrated Women*. "Call me when you want me at your side." Kwan never made that phone call. Then, on October 19—just four months before the Olympics—Kwan did what some people might call the unthinkable. She fired Carroll, who had been her coach, confidant, and support since she was 11 years old. Over the years, Kwan and Carroll became so close that at press conferences they often started talking at the same time saying the exact same thing. During the 1998 Olympics, they even showed up wearing matching outfits. After all the years Carroll had invested in Kwan, many people wondered, "Why now? Why this year?"

Theories about Kwan's sudden decision varied, but everyone was confused. When Nichols heard the news, she was stunned. "Letting the choreographer go is one thing," she said in *Sports Illustrated Women*. "But the coach!" Some believed Kwan was just trying to shake things up a bit, get the excitement hot. Skating legend Fleming speculated in *Sports Illustrated Women*, "Kwan wants the challenge of doing something new. When the pressure's really the hottest, that's when she comes alive." Kwan somewhat agreed with this opinion. "My dad always tells me I have to be up against a wall to fight back," she said in the same article. Still others claimed Kwan fired Carroll because he thought she was spending too much time with her boyfriend, Brad Ference, a defenseman for the NHL's Florida Panthers. But Kwan denied this idea, insisting the opposite was true, that she never had time to see him. "As I've gotten older, I've gotten more independent, and I think for myself," Kwan said, according to Gérard Châtaigneau and Steve Milton's book, *Figure Skating Now: Olympic and World Stars*. "And that's the way it should be."

On October 23, Kwan got pummeled with questions during a press conference at Skate America in Colorado Springs, Colorado. "I love Frank very much," she said. "But maybe it's just better now to skate alone, listen to myself, and see where it gets me."

At Skate America, Danny stood in Carroll's usual spot. Kwan just wanted to have someone there. In her long program, she cut a triple toe loop to a double, and a double axel to a single. The real star of the competition was 16-year-old Sarah Hughes. She skated confidently, landing a difficult triple salchow–triple loop combination. Her program was superior in almost every necessary element—music, choreography, footwork, spins, jumps, and speed. At the end of her long program, she arched into a layback spin that brought the crowd to its feet. When the scores popped up, the crowd booed. Five out of seven judges placed Kwan first.

One week later, Kwan and Hughes again faced off at Skate Canada in Saskatoon, Saskatchewan. The programs were much the same, but this time, with different results. Kwan fell twice in her long program. Irina Slutskaya, who hadn't skated at Skate America, two-footed a landing. Hughes skated cleanly. When the scores came in, Hughes got her deserved gold, Slutskaya took silver, and Kwan finished with a bronze—the lowest finish she had taken since 1996.

There is a saying in figure skating: the ice is slippery. In other words, anything can happen. Kwan was the picture of grace under pressure. Perhaps the trips and troubles were all part of her plan to bounce back and steal Olympic gold. When she took first at Nationals, it seemed as though she was all set up to finally capture her dream.

Three solid skaters led the American team at the 2002 Olympics in Salt Lake City, Utah. Leading the pack was Kwan, the ice-skating legend of her time. Sasha Cohen—whose amazing flexibility mesmerized crowds—was quickly skating up the ranks. She planned to raise the stakes by attempting a quadruple salchow in her Olympic program. No woman had ever completed a quadruple jump in a competition. Then, there was young sensation Sarah Hughes, who didn't yet have a driver's license but could cruise on a pair of skates. Her steady rise to Olympic contender in just three years couldn't have been planned more precisely. She covered the rink with more speed than both Kwan and Cohen and tackled her jumps and spins with explosive energy. As an overall skater, she was more consistent than Cohen and was capable of causing quite an upset at the Olympic Games. Who would end up on the podium was anybody's guess. But did anyone want it worse than Michelle Kwan?

On the night of the short program, the air was charged with excitement and anticipation. Hughes got ready to skate.

She clasped her hands in prayer before taking the ice. She had a slow, nervous start and barely hung onto her triple flip, but she hit every element. At the end of the program, she clapped for herself and pumped her arms in the air. She had gotten through the first Olympic run with flying colors. After Hughes, Cohen skated onto the ice. The 17-year-old had missed the 2000–2001 season because of a back injury but forged her way back to finish second to Kwan at Nationals. Speeding across the ice with energy and enthusiasm, she skated quicker and smoother than Hughes, and her spirals would rival Kwan's.

However, most people had their eyes focused on the top two rivals—Slutskaya and Kwan. Slutskaya's program, skated to music by Schubert, was technically sharp but lacked spark. Her jumps were smooth, and her combination spins and layback were magnificent. But Kwan was ready to ignite the whole package. She was thrilled to skate on her home turf. And despite the year's turmoil, she was ready for the moment.

Frenzied shouts showered down from the stands as Kwan skated out onto the ice. The noise didn't distract her. She was inspired. This year, she wouldn't hold back or be cautious as she had been in 1998. She let it all go. Her showmanship was brilliant, even though she under-rotated her triple flip, which dropped her technical score a bit. At one point in the program, she spiraled across more than half the rink, her arms gracefully extended. When the music ended, she saw dozens of U.S. flags rippling in the stands. On the way off the ice, she picked up a stuffed animal that had been thrown onto the ice and sat down in Kiss and Cry to wait for her marks. A stream of 5.9s for artistry spread across the scoreboard. She had edged out Slutskaya for first place, Cohen finished third, and Hughes dropped to fourth.

The night ended as everyone had expected, with Kwan on top. "I'm proud to be an American, and I tried to skate from my heart, tried to make Americans proud," Kwan said, according to SportsIllustrated.com. "It was an incredible moment for me."

But she was only a fraction of the way to Olympic gold. Ahead of her loomed the more important freeskate, and the ice was slippery. Anything could happen.

The night of the long program, Kwan and the world were stunned by an unexpected twist. Hughes, who finished fourth in the short program, had the skate of a lifetime. She attempted the most difficult technical program ever at the women's competition. Aside from one minor technical flaw—turning a lutz into an easier flip, called a flutz—she skated it magnificently, landing all seven triple jumps. At the end, her eyes glistened with excitement and surprise.

Her marks set the bar high. Kwan would have to skate a flawless program. If she did it, she could hold on to the gold. She started out strong, flowing along in her exquisite style. Suddenly, the unthinkable happened—she crashed on a triple jump. The rest of her program was smooth, but the fall cost her dearly. The other contenders bobbled as well. It was the biggest upset in skating history; Hughes catapulted from fourth to win the gold medal. Slutskaya stayed in second place. Cohen, who did not attempt her quadruple jump, fell to fourth. Kwan took the bronze—two huge spots short of her lifetime goal. The disappointment must have been unbearable, but Kwan handled it with the grace and dignity she had become famous for.

After the Olympics, Hughes decided not to compete in the 2002 World Championships in Nagano, Japan. There, Slutskaya finally won out over her long-time rival and snatched the world title. Kwan won silver—two back-to-back bitter defeats. Many skaters would have bowed out of competitive skating at this point. But Kwan was not about to give up. At the 2006 Olympics, she would be 25—still young enough to compete. She forged on and won her seventh U.S. Championship in 2003. At the 2003 Worlds, she became the first skater to recapture the world title three times in a career. In 2004, she won her eighth gold medal at Nationals. At Worlds, she took the bronze. Nevertheless, her drop at the World Championships did not signal a decline.

Michelle Kwan looks on as fellow American Sarah Hughes is awarded the gold medal at the 2002 Winter Olympics in Salt Lake City. Although the favorite to win going into the Games, Kwan earned the bronze medal, finishing behind Russian skater Irina Slutskaya and 17-year-old Hughes.

The following year, she became a nine-time U.S. champion, an amazing record. But she faltered again at the 2005 World Championships, finishing in fourth place, missing the podium for the first time in nine years.

Going into the 2005–2006 Olympic season, many questions must have plagued her mind. Was her finish at Worlds a sign that she should quit competitive skating? Could she really give up her dream of Olympic gold? She had fought her way back before. Perhaps with her back against the wall again, a fight was just what she needed.

10

End of a Dream

Coming in fourth at the 2005 Worlds in Moscow, Russia, was a learning experience for Kwan. It was her first time skating under the new scoring system. The system was developed after the 2002 Olympic figure skating scandal in Salt Lake City.

Later in March, Kwan competed in the U.S. Figure Skating Challenge in Tampa, Florida. The event was judged using the old 6.0 system, so Kwan was back in her comfort zone, and it showed. She skated her program to "Bolero" with passion and spark, attacking jump after jump. In the highlight of the final footwork sequence, Kwan flew across the ice in twists and turns. Her first-place finish was just what she needed to boost her confidence for the coming Olympic season.

The competition had a whole different feel to Kwan than Worlds. Perhaps the change had something to do with the weather. She traded in the below-zero temperatures in Moscow for the sunny and sultry weather of Florida. Kwan admitted she was tempted to skip practice and go lie out by the pool. "This is

Michelle Kwan performs a routine in 2005 at the U.S. Figure Skating Challenge in Boston. Although she gave a shaky performance, Kwan managed to win the event due to her popularity. Unlike most other skating competitions, this event allowed the fans to decide who should win.

what I like! I'm a California girl," she said in an article by Kwan Wojdyla on the U.S. Figure Skating Web site.

In early October, Kwan strained a ligament in her right hip during practice. Even though she tried to keep going, the pain forced her to quit practicing. The pain was so intense she couldn't even get out of the bathtub. Even after two weeks off, just stepping on the ice hurt. Before long, Kwan started to panic. She thought her season was over.

Her doctor assured her that she would make a compete recovery in plenty of time to train for the Olympics. She withdrew from several competitions, including the 2005 International Figure Skating Challenge, the 2005 Skate America, and the Cup of China in November. As the ligament healed, she gradually increased her ice time. At first, she was allowed only 30 minutes on the ice. By December, she was up to two hour-long sessions a day. But that was still short of the three hours a day she usually trained.

At a press conference in December, reporters asked Kwan if she would be skating at the upcoming U.S. Championships in January. "The pain is manageable," she said. "I can push as hard as I need to for Nationals. I just have to be careful how much I can push." Remembering the stress fracture she came out of the 1998 Nationals with, Kwan stayed optimistic. "I've done this before," she said.

By the middle of December, Kwan was back in her normal routine and skating well. Then on December 17, she pulled her right groin muscle during practice. She wouldn't be able to skate at Nationals after all. On January 4, she announced her decision to withdraw from the U.S. Championships but held on to hope that she would still be able to compete at the 2006 Olympics in Torino (Turin), Italy. She planned to submit a formal petition to the U.S. Figure Skating International Committee for one of the three ladies' spots on the 2006 U.S. Olympic figure skating team.

"I am deeply disappointed that I will not be at Nationals," Kwan said in an article on the U.S. Figure Skating Web site. "It's always been my favorite event, especially in an Olympic year, and I was really looking forward to competing. . . . Both my doctor and I feel that I can get back to that level and be completely ready for the Olympics. For that reason, I am petitioning for a spot on the team."

According to the U.S. Figure Skating athlete selection rules for the 2006 Olympic Games, the champions of each division at the 2006 U.S. Championships would automatically be nominated to the team. The remaining spots would be determined by the U.S. Figure Skating International Committee. A skater who was unable to skate in competitions due to injury or illness could file a petition for one of those spots. The committee's decisions would be based on the skater's performance at the 2006 U.S. Championships, the 2005 Grand Prix Final, the 2005 World Championships, the 2005 Four Continents Championships, and several others. The only one of these events that Kwan had participated in was 2005 Worlds, where she placed fourth.

For any other skater, fourth place at the previous year's World Championships probably wouldn't be enough to earn a spot on the Olympic team. But Kwan had a reputation—eight consecutive U.S. Championship titles, nine in all, and five world titles. She is the most decorated figure skater in U.S. history. Kwan probably knew she would have no trouble getting on the team. Of course, this decision would mean that one of the medalists from the U.S. Championships would get bumped off the team, probably bronze medalist Emily Hughes, younger sister of Sarah Hughes. Kwan was not a stranger to that experience, either. In 1994, she was the one who got bumped for Nancy Kerrigan.

Later in January, the U.S. Figure Skating International Committee and the USOC announced that Michelle Kwan, Sasha Cohen, and Kimmie Meissner were nominated to the 2006 Olympic Team. Cohen and Meissner had placed first and second at the U.S. Championships in St. Louis, Missouri. Emily Hughes would be the first alternate. "The International Committee considered all of the relevant information and picked the best possible U.S. Olympic Team to represent the United States in Torino," International Committee chair Bob Horen said. "We believe that Sasha, Kimmie, and Michelle will compete in a manner that will make our country proud." Kwan was on her way to her fourth Olympics, with one more chance to catch the gold medal.

AN OLYMPIC FAREWELL

Less than 24 hours after Kwan arrived in Italy, her third Olympic venture turned topsy-turvy. On the night of February 10, Kwan marched in the opening ceremonies. The next morning, she took to the ice for practice. Strangely, she felt stiff. The long plane ride and all that marching the night before took a toll on her body. As she came out of her second jump, a triple flip, she landed on two feet. Immediately, she knew she had hurt something. She tried another jump and fell hard. Tears filled her eyes as she skated to the sidelines, leaving practice 15 minutes early. Kwan hoped that with some therapy, the stiffness would go away. But by evening, the pain had worsened. It was so severe, she couldn't even sleep.

At 2:15 in the morning, she called the team doctor, who hurried to see her in the Olympic Village. He quickly diagnosed her injury as a pulled groin muscle. With little time to heal, her chances to compete were doomed. Apparently, more than just a jump had crashed that morning on the ice. Her dreams of getting an Olympic gold medal tumbled with it.

Kwan knew that she wouldn't be able to give 100 percent out on the ice. She had made a promise to the Olympic Committee that if for any reason she couldn't skate her best, she would give up her spot on the team. Immediately, a call was placed to the home of 17-year-old Emily Hughes. By 7:30 the next morning, the U.S. team had made a formal application for replacement. Fewer than three hours later, the substitution was approved. Although withdrawing was one of the toughest decisions Kwan ever had to make, she knew it was the right one.

On February 12, 2006, Michelle Kwan announces her withdrawal from the Torino Winter Olympics due to a severe groin injury. "It's always been a dream to win the Olympics," Kwan said during the press conference. "But I've learned it's not about the gold, it's about the spirit of it and about the sport itself."

Once again proving to be an ultimate class act, Kwan chose to leave Torino and go back home to Los Angeles. She didn't want to be a distraction to the competition. She would bid the Olympics a fond farewell, without its crowning achievement. "It's not all about the gold," she gracefully stated through her tears, according to an article by Mark Starr on *Newsweek*'s Web site. "It's about sport. I have no regrets. I tried my best and if I didn't win the gold, it's OK. I had a great career."

Undoubtedly, never has an athlete's sorrow been felt by so many people. Just before Kwan announced her painful decision, U.S. Olympic Committee chairman Peter Ueberroth made an extraordinary introduction. "Michelle Kwan means more to the

United States Olympic Committee than maybe any athlete that has ever performed [for it]," he said.

Later that day, two planes passed in the sky. In one plane, Emily Hughes's Olympic dream was just beginning. In the other, Michelle Kwan's dream was coming to an end. Kwan's competitive career has probably drawn to a close. She will be 29 at the 2010 Winter Olympics in Vancouver, and her body isn't as indestructible as it once was, having suffered two groin injuries in a month. When asked if she will continue to compete, Kwan answered, "I can't think past right now," according to an Associated Press article by Nancy Armour. Still, Kwan knows her limits and when to say when. As she said in Edward Z. Epstein's *Born to Skate*, "I always tell myself I'm not going to do this until I'm thirty. That's way too long. If you can't show your best on the ice, why show it? I want to be the best and walk out. I don't want to be skating when I'm going downhill."

However, she performed in the 2006 Champions on Ice tour in the spring and summer. (In August, she underwent elective arthroscopic surgery to repair a torn labrum in her right hip, an old injury from the 2004–2005 season.) Although she will not be competing in the 2006–2007 figure skating season, Michelle will likely continue skating as long as she can. "Skating is in my heart, not my head," she said in her autobiography, *Heart of a Champion*. Michelle Kwan will probably go down in history as the greatest female skater of all time. Even though she never captured that Olympic gold medal, she has proven time and time again she has the heart of a true champion. She is a leader, a glowing example of good sportsmanship, and a role model for young skaters and athletes alike.

GOODWILL AMBASSADOR

On November 9, 2006, Kwan, who is currently studying political science and international affairs at the University of Denver, was chosen for some extraordinary on-the-job experience.

Secretary of State Condoleezza Rice appointed her as a public diplomatic envoy for the United States. According to Rice, the determined skater who won her first world title at the age of fifteen has lived a "deeply American story" and is admired by many. Kwan's job as a non-salaried goodwill ambassador is part of the State Department's Education and Cultural Affairs program to reach young people around the world who have been overexposed to hate propaganda directed against the United States. U.S. officials believe Kwan's patriotism and reputation as a world-class skater will help improve the nation's image overseas. Always proud to represent her country, Kwan is looking forward to her new role.

CHRONOLOGY

1980 *July 7* Michelle Kwan is born in Torrance, California, to Danny and Estella Kwan.

1985 Michelle laces up her first pair of skates and takes to the ice; shortly after her first skating experience, she starts taking lessons.

1988 Michelle watches the 1988 Winter Olympics and sees Brian Boitano win Olympic gold; her dream of becoming an Olympic skater is born; Danny hires private skating teacher Derek James for Michelle and her sister Karen.

1992 Michelle becomes a junior skater; wins a gold medal at the Southwest Pacific Regional Championships; wins bronze at the Pacific Coast Sectionals, which qualifies her to compete at Junior Nationals.

1992 *December* Michelle finishes ninth at the Junior U.S. Championships in Orlando, Florida.

1993 Michelle becomes a senior lady; takes first place at the Gardena Spring Trophy in Ortisei, Italy; wins a gold medal at the Olympic Festival in San Antonio, Texas.

1994 *January* Nancy Kerrigan is clubbed in the knee before Nationals; Michelle wins silver at the U.S. Championships, qualifying her for the 1994 Olympic Team.

1994 *February* Kwan goes to Lillehammer, Norway, as an Olympic alternate.

1994 *March* Kwan finishes eighth at the World Championships and secures two spots for the American skating team at the 1995

Worlds; takes silver at the U.S. Pro-Am Championships.

1995 *January*   Despite a flawless program, Kwan finishes fourth at the U.S. Championships; after Nationals, she makes her transformation from sweet kid to seductive Salome.

1995 *October*   In her first time skating as Salome, Kwan beats reigning world champion Lu Chen of China for first place at Skate America in Detroit.

1996 *January*   Kwan wins her first U.S. Championship in San Jose, California.

TIMELINE

July 7, 1980
Michelle Kwan is born in Torrance, California, to Danny and Estella Kwan.

January 1994
Kwan wins silver at the U.S. Championships, qualifying her for the 1994 Olympic Team.

February 1994
Kwan goes to Lillehammer, Norway, as an Olympic alternate.

January 1996
Kwan wins her first U.S. Championship in San Jose, California.

March 1996
Kwan wins the gold medal at the Worlds, becoming the youngest skater to win the world title.

1980

1998

1985
Kwan laces up her first pair of skates and takes to the ice.

1993
Kwan becomes a senior lady; wins a gold medal at the Olympic Festival in San Antonio, Texas.

December 1992
Kwan finishes ninth at the Junior U.S. Championships in Orlando, Florida.

January 1998
At the U.S. Championships, Kwan makes skating history with seven perfect 6.0s in her short program and eight 6.0s in her long program, winning her second gold medal at Nationals.

1996 *March* Kwan wins the gold medal at the Worlds, becoming the youngest skater to win the world title.

1997 *January* Fourteen-year-old Tara Lipinski edges out Kwan for gold at Nationals and Worlds; Kwan finishes second at both events.

1998 *January* At the U.S. Championships, Kwan makes skating history with seven perfect 6.0s in her short program and eight 6.0s in her long program, winning her second gold medal at Nationals.

March 2000
Kwan wins gold at the World Championships, becoming the first female skater to recapture the world title twice in her career.

March 2003
Kwan wins the gold medal at Worlds, making her the first female skater to recapture the title three times in her career.

January 2006
Kwan drops out of the U.S. Championships due to a pulled groin muscle; she petitions the U.S. Figure Skating International Committee for a spot on the 2006 Olympic team and is nominated to the team; after less than 24 hours in Torino, Kwan pulls another groin muscle in practice and has to withdraw from the Olympic competition.

2000

2006

January 2002
Kwan takes her sixth gold medal at the U.S. Championships.

February 2002
After ending up in first place after the short program, Michelle finishes with a heartbreaking bronze at the Winter Olympics in Salt Lake City, Utah; 16-year-old Sarah Hughes of America wins the gold and Irina Slutskaya of Russia takes silver.

January 2005
Kwan becomes a nine-time U.S. champion; in March, she finishes fourth at Worlds, her first time to miss the podium in nine years.

1998 *February* Kwan wins silver at the Winter Olympics in Nagano, Japan; 15-year-old American Tara Lipinski takes the gold, becoming the youngest skater to win Olympic gold.

1999 *September* Kwan starts college at the University of California, Los Angeles.

1999 *January* Kwan wins gold at the U.S. Championships.

1999 *March* Kwan takes silver at the World Championships.

2000 *January* Kwan wins her fifth National Championship.

2000 *March* Kwan wins gold at the World Championships, becoming the first female skater to recapture the world title twice in her career.

2001 *January* Kwan captures her fourth consecutive, and fifth in all, national title.

2001 *March* Again, Kwan takes gold at the Worlds.

2001 *June* Kwan fires choreographer Lori Nichols and hires Sarah Kawahara to take her place.

2001 *October* Kwan fires coach Frank Carroll after more than 10 years working together; shortly after, she ends up with bronze at Skate Canada, her lowest finish since 1996.

2002 *January* Kwan takes her sixth gold medal at the U.S. Championships.

2002 *February* After ending up in first place after the short program, Kwan finishes with a heartbreaking bronze at the Winter Olympics in Salt Lake City, Utah; 16-year-old Sarah Hughes of America wins the gold and Irina Slutskaya of Russia takes silver.

2002 *March* Kwan finishes with silver at the

Worlds, edged out by longtime rival Irina Slutskaya.

2003 *January* Kwan wins her seventh U.S. Championship.

2003 *March* Kwan wins the gold medal at Worlds, making her the first female skater to recapture the title three times in her career.

2004 *January* Again, Kwan wins Nationals, her eighth gold medal.

2004 *March* Kwan finishes with bronze at the World Championships.

2005 *January* Kwan becomes a nine-time U.S. champion; in March, she finishes fourth at the Worlds, her first time to miss the podium in nine years.

2006 *January* Kwan drops out of the U.S. Championships due to a pulled groin muscle; she petitions the U.S. Figure Skating International Committee for a spot on the 2006 Olympic team and is nominated to the team; after less than 24 hours in Torino, Kwan pulls another groin muscle in practice and has to withdraw from the Olympic competition.

GLOSSARY

axel—A jump in figure skating from the outer forward edge of one skate with 1½ turns taken in the air and a return to the outer backward edge of the other skate.

Kiss and Cry—The area where figure skaters sit to learn their scores.

lutz—A backward figureskating jump with a takeoff from the outside edge of one skate followed by a full turn in the air and a landing on the outside edge of the other skate.

salchow—A figureskating jump with a takeoff from the back inside edge of one skate followed by one or more full turns in the air and a landing on the back outside edge of the opposite skate.

BIBLIOGRAPHY

Armour, Nancy. "Kwan's Olympic Career Ends on a Sad Note."
   Associated Press, Breitbart.com. http://www.breitbart.com/
   news/2006/02/12/D8FNQ1083.html.

Brennan, Christine. *Edge of Glory*. New York: Penguin Books,
   1999.

Châtaigneau, Gérard, and Steve Milton. *Figure Skating Now:
   Olympic and World Stars*. Buffalo, NY: Firefly Books, 2003.

Epstein, Edward Z. *Born to Skate: The Michelle Kwan Story*. New
   York: Ballantine Books, 1997.

Hines, James R. *Figure Skating: A History*. Chicago: University of
   Illinois Press, 2006.

Kwan, Michelle. *Michelle Kwan: Heart of a Champion, an Autobiography*. New York: Scholastic, 1997.

———. *The Winning Attitude*. New York: Hyperion Books for
   Children, 1999.

Lovitt, Chip. *Skating for the Gold: Michelle Kwan and Tara Lipinski*. New York: Pocket Books, 1997.

Magic Memories on Ice III (video).

Smith, Russell Scott. "Whither the Queen?" *Sports Illustrated
   Women*. http://sportsillustrated.com.cnn.com/siwomen/
   february/queen.

SportsIllustrated.com. "Smooth on Ice: Kwan Wins Short Program Over Rival Slutskaya." http://sportsillustrated.cnn.
   com/olympics/2002/figure_skating/news/2002/02/19/
   womens_short_program_ap.

Starr, Mark. "Homeward Bound." Newsweek Web Exclusive, February 12, 2006. http://www.msnbc.msn.com/id/11308215/
   site/newsweek.

2002 Salt Lake City (video).

U.S. Figure Skating Online. "Athlete Bio—Michelle Kwan." http://
   www.usfigureskating.org/AthleteBio.asp?id=2267.

U.S. Figure Skating Online. "Cohen, Meissner, Kwan Nominated
   to 2006 U.S. Olympic Figure Skating Team." January 14, 2006.
   http://www.usfigureskating.org/Story.asp?id=32534.

U.S. Figure Skating Online. "Michelle Kwan Withdraws from 2006 State Farm U.S. Figure Skating Championships Due to Injury; Will Petition for Spot on U.S. Olympic Team." January 4, 2006. http://www.usfigureskating.org/Story.asp?id=32500.

Wojdyla, Michelle. "Athletes Meet the Press at Marshalls Challenge." U.S. Figure Skating Online. December 10, 2005. http://www.usfigureskating.org/Story.asp?id=32302.

———. "Bringing Down the House at Marshalls U.S. Figure Skating Challenge." U.S. Figure Skating Online. March 29, 2005. http://www.usfigureskating.org/Story.asp?id=29424.

FURTHER READING

BOOKS

Epstein, Edward Z. *Born to Skate: The Michelle Kwan Story.* New York: Ballantine Books, 1997.

Kwan, Michelle. *Michelle Kwan: Heart of a Champion, an Autobiography.* New York: Scholastic, 1997.

Kwan, Michelle. *The Winning Attitude.* New York: Hyperion Books for Children, 1999.

Lovitt, Chip. *Skating for the Gold: Michelle Kwan and Tara Lipinski.* New York: Pocket Books, 1997.

WEB SITES

Kristi Yamaguchi's Always Dream Foundation
http://www.alwaysdream.org

NBC Olympics
http://www.nbcolympics.com

The Official Web Site of the Olympic Movement
http://www.olympic.org

The Official Site of the U.S. Olympic Team
http://www.usolympicteam.com

U.S. Figure Skating
http://www.usfigureskating.org

PHOTO CREDITS

INDEX

ABOUT
THE AUTHOR

RACHEL A. KOESTLER-GRACK has worked with nonfiction books as an editor and writer since 1999. During her career, she has worked extensively with historical topics, ranging from the Middle Ages to the colonial era to the civil rights movement. In addition, she has written numerous biographies on a variety of historical and contemporary figures. Rachel lives with her husband and daughter on a hobby farm near Glencoe, Minnesota.